# Prayer Therapy of Jesus

Doris Gaines Rapp, Ph.D.

*Prayer Therapy of Jesus*                                                   Doris Gaines Rapp, Ph.D.

# Prayer Therapy of Jesus

### Doris Gaines Rapp, Ph.D.

**Author of**

*Waiting for Jesus in a Can't Wait World*
Advent

and

*Lent is for Giving In, Not Giving Up*
Lent

Daniel's House Publishing

2nd Edition Copyright © 2014 Doris Gaines Rapp, Ph.D.

Copyright © 2000, 2001 by Doris Gaines Rapp, Ph.D.
under the title *A Magnificat for a New Millennium*

This Second Edition has been edited and new material added.

All rights reserved.
No part of this book may be reproduced, stored in a retrieval system, or transmitted by any means, electronic, mechanical, photocopying, recording, or otherwise, without written permission from the author.

Library of Congress Control Number: 2014916902
ISBN: 978-0-9637200-5-4 (sc)
ISBN: 978-0-9637200-7-8 (iBook)

Dedicated to my husband Bill who is always patient with my writing, and to my parents, Dan and Mildred Gaines, who introduced me to God. I also dedicate this book on prayer to all my children: Vicki, Donna, James, Vonn, Kathleen, and Amanda. I pray that you will have an exquisite adventure in your own prayer life. Nothing is more thrilling for me, than to watch the will of God unfold in your lives.

**Dr. Doris Gaines Rapp, Ph.D.** is a writer by birth, and psychologist and teacher by education and experiences. She writes on the topic of Prayer Therapy at www.prayertherapyrapp.blogspot.com. There is a new post each Monday. Rapp is a speaker and also writes fiction. Her fictional characters live in several centuries. All of her works have a Christian basis. The former Counseling Center Director of Taylor University, Upland, and Bethel College, Mishawaka, IN, she currently writes full time. She and her pastor husband live in Indiana.

www.dorisgainesrapp.com
www.dorisgainesrapp.blogspot.com
www.prayertherapyrapp.blogspot.com
https://www.amazon.com/author/dorisgainesrapp
Facebook.com/pages/Doris-Gaines-Rapp-Author-Page

*Prayer Therapy of Jesus*             Doris Gaines Rapp, Ph.D.

## Introduction

"Christianity just doesn't work," some moan. Or, they don't know how to "make it work." It seems that the entire world is seeking a spiritual awakening. Some are turning from early training to other religions and experiences. They think they can find a genie who will work *for* them.

Christianity is not a religion that serves us. It is a personal relationship, made possible by the blood of Jesus. It is about grace sufficient to save even you and me. It is about coming along side others as they learn to *link* with Christ. It is the privilege of serving God, not of him serving us, even if the job is wiping his feet with our tears. It is about a walk along life's road as it winds through shadowed valleys and rises from time to time to the high mountains, where we can nearly reach out and touch the outstretched hand of God, and walking yet on, on our way home.

We have all prayed. My guess is, even those who don't believe in God, have argued with Him about his existence. Since we cannot argue with someone who isn't there, even their argument becomes testimony to his presence. As a psychologist, I have talked with people who claim they no longer believe in God, but then challenge me to change their mind. They long to believe, but are wandering in a desert of despair, lost and alone.

Those of us who do pray often lose heart when we don't see evidence of our prayers being answered in the way we want them answered. We assume it is God's fault—he has chosen to not listen or respond to our prayers. Perhaps, (1) we are not praying to be of use to him. We are praying for him to serve us. (2) We are not praying for our current specific needs, "our daily bread," as Jesus taught us. We are praying for an accumulation—the entire bakery.

*Prayer Therapy of Jesus*                          Doris Gaines Rapp, Ph.D.

This book is a step-by-step training manual in prayer. It can become your awakening to a new relationship with God, an exquisite adventure. By learning to pray to serve the Lord, it can be our personal ministry. Christ came to heal both the body and the spirit. Some are healed here on earth and some are healed through a resurrection healing—both are divine healing.

Throughout the first part of the book, where I have identified each part of a prayer using the Prayer Therapy model, I am including a full devotional. Many of us are called on to give devotions at an event. While we will have covered the elements of Prayer Therapy in this training guide, I want you to see how to take a theme and a scripture, and develop an entire devotion from the concepts of Prayer Therapy. You are free to use the devotions printed here at gatherings in which you are called on to participate. Please acknowledge the source: "First written by Doris Gaines Rapp, Ph.D. on (the date at the end of the devotion) when it was posted to Dr. Rapp's blog, www.prayertherapyrapp.blogspot.com."

Remember:

1. The scripture you select will inform the topic of the devotion and the converse is true. The topic of your devotion will determine the appropriate scripture.
2. The body of the devotion is the message, the single thought you want to leave with the reader or listener.
3. Using this model, the prayer will be based on Prayer Therapy, as described throughout this book.

For this introduction, I am including a full devotional from my blog, www.prayertherapyrapp.blogspot.com, on Resurrection Healing. A new entry is posted each Monday.

## Resurrection Healing

Paul said . . ."Concerning this I implored the Lord three times that it might leave me. And He has said to me, 'My grace is sufficient for you, for power is perfected in weakness.' Most gladly, therefore, I will rather boast about my weaknesses, so that the power of Christ may dwell in me. Therefore I am well content with weaknesses, with insults, with distresses, with persecutions, with difficulties, for Christ's sake; for when I am weak, then I am strong." 2 Corinthians 12: 8-10

Have you heard the painful accusation, "They are sick because they didn't have enough faith in God to let Him heal them? How cruel. Where does the Bible say, if we have enough faith we will be perfect? As Paul tells us, God's power is perfected in our weaknesses. Some are healed in the body and some are given power to do God's will in spite of their affliction, to prove *His* strength.

All will be made perfect on the Day of Resurrection. For most Christians that is understood as, we will be made perfect when we come into the presence of God, whether that be when we die or when the Lord Returns. This, however, is not a few sentences on a centuries' old argument over when Jesus will return, or when the faithful will be raised from the dead. I believe He will return, the timing is totally up to God and my opinion will not cause Him to tarry one moment or speed His return by a nanosecond. We will be given the power to do God's will here on earth, regardless of our physical limitations. Then, the world will see the might of God in spite of our disabilities. We will be made perfect—have resurrection healing—when we cast off our earth-bound body and soar to the throne of God. Do not be discouraged if you cannot run fast, preach eloquently, sing beautifully, or even get up off the floor once you have sat down. God has a plan for you that will be fulfilled when you give yourself over to His power in your life. Let us pray:

"Holy Father, Abba, Daddy, I bow before you and your plan for my life. You are Holy; I am not worthy of having you direct my life, but I give it over to you willingly. Whatever I do in your name, it will be by your grace and power. Please, accept this flawed life I give you and use it to fulfill whatever you have in mind. Forgive me when I have given away your blessings because they didn't fit into my busy schedule. May this be the day when excuses stop and I accept your power to perfect my weaknesses. I am healed when I believe in your power to heal in your time, and I let you decide what needs to be healed in me: my body, soul, emotions, relationships, career or flaws I'm not even aware of. In the name of your son Jesus, I pray. Amen"
Doris

Posted and copyrighted Doris Gaines Rapp at www.prayertherapyrapp@blogspot.com on 8-18-14.

## Chapter 1

**Prayer Therapy**

Pray intentionally, specifically, and watch the glory of God burst forth in your life! God will answer those prayers specifically in his own way.

Prayer Therapy is a form of prayer in which you pray selectively for release from the specific pain in your life that harms you, so God can answer specifically. The disciples asked Jesus to teach them how to pray and he gave them The Lord's Prayer.

Many of us suffer from ill health, depression and other illnesses that have a physical connection. Jesus's prayer provides a way to teach us how to pray for release from the negative elements that harm us. For us to learn to pray therapeutically, prescriptively, specifically, I have labeled the various phrases of the Lord's Prayer. Knowing what each segment means, we can learn to put the prayer into our own words and bury their meaning in our heart.

On the following page, I have written the Lord's Prayer in segments or phrases and have identified each of their meanings. The passage is from the New Testament book of Matthew.

*Prayer Therapy of Jesus*                                Doris Gaines Rapp, Ph.D.

| Matthew 6: 9-12 | King James Version | New International Version |
|---|---|---|
| 1.) Acknowledgement: | "Our Father, which art in Heaven," | "Our Father in Heaven, |
| 2.) Reverence/Worship: | hallowed be thy name. | hallowed be your name. |
| 3.) Pray for Christ's return: | Thy kingdom come, | Your kingdom come |
| 4.) Surrender: | thy will be done in earth as it is in Heaven. | your will be done on earth as it is in Heaven. |
| 5.) Petition: | Give us this day our daily bread. | Give us this day our daily bread. |
| 6.) Prayer for forgiveness: | And forgive us our <u>debts</u>, (trespasses) as we forgive our <u>debtors</u> (those who trespass against us.) | Forgive us our debts, as we also have forgiven our debtors. |
| 7.) Deliverance from our sins | And lead us not into temptation but deliver us from evil. | And lead us not into temptation but deliver us from the evil one." |
| 8.) Acknowledge His Omnipresence | For thine is the kingdom, | |
| 9.) Acknowledge His Omnipotence | and the power, | |
| 10.) Relinquishing credit Back to God | and the glory, forever. | |
| 11.) Closing | Amen." | |
| 12.) *Claiming Christ's power | *In the name of Jesus Christ, or by the power of Jesus Christ. | |
| 13.) *Prayer Therapy | A specific, personal petition. | |
| 14.) *Intercession | A specific prayer for another. | |
| 15.) *Secret Prayer | | *Identifies items not mentioned in Matthew 6. |

Prayer Therapy falls within the fifth segment of the prayer, labeled "Petition," the section where we pray for specific needs. "Needs" can be "daily bread" or freedom from anger, jealously or other negative emotions. William Parker and Elaine St. John wrote a wonderful book, published in 1957, titled, *Prayer Can Change Your Life*.

In Parker and St. John's book they described their scientific study in which they investigated the effectiveness of prayer. In the nine-month study, most of the participants improved their health by a method of specific praying: clearly naming negative emotions and not just random praying.

Negative emotions make us weak and, over time, they can make us ill. I am not saying, "It's all in your head." But, if your head isn't in the game of health, your score will fall like a concrete basketball.

Random prayers had no effect at all on health improvement. A random prayer would be the type we whisper as we run out the door in the morning.

- "Help me to do well on the test today."
- "Help me to get along well with my boss."
- "Let this day be better than yesterday."

A specific prayer follows the same template as taught by our Lord, as outlined below. It includes a request that God release us from specific negative emotions which rob us of our mental and physical health, energy and wellbeing.

I am not suggesting you attempt to "cure" your own physical or emotional problems without professional help. You may need to see a psychologist, counselor, and/or physician. Prayer Therapy can accompany proper psychological and medical treatment, if needed, or stand alone.

In my private practice, I have witnessed patients' emotional health improve, as well as their relationships with others, through praying for specific needs. The specific need of which I speak is "release of the captives."

"Release of the captives," might sound like something out of a spy novel or a swash-buckling movie. It is not. We are all captive, at one time or another, to certain negative feelings, emotions and/or thoughts. What we feel or think can actually make us physically ill. Negative emotions can also rob us of positive relationships with others. Let me tell you what I mean.

A sincere Evangelical Christian man came in seeking therapy for depression. As we talked about his life and family, he described his work in his church and how inadequate he felt. He kept repeating that his parents had not been Christians and he had not been reared in the larger Christian community. To him, that was his whole problem. "They are good people, but they did not raise me in the church."

He felt cheated and strongly believed if he had been reared in the church, he would not have his current problems or depression. That may have been quite true, but it was also assuredly accurate that the short-comings of his parents were in his past. His problems were in the present.

"Do you pray for your parents?" I asked him.

His response was as expected. "Yes, of course I pray for them."

"Do you ever thank God for giving you the parents that he did? Remember, in all things be thankful."

"No," he said he did not thank God for giving him his parents. To the contrary, he often questioned God, and sometimes very angrily, he admitted. "God, why did you place me in this home with these parents?" He didn't think he could ever thank God for his parents. He had longed for a different mom and dad for so long, he couldn't see how being thankful for the very mother and father he had, would be helpful.

"So, God made a mistake?" I asked.

"No, but I haven't thanked God for them either."

You guessed it. That became his prescription. He was to pray three times a day, in praise to God for his wisdom in giving him the parents he had given him.

He really didn't want to give thanks for his parents at first. But, since he knew, in all things he was to be grateful, he complied with the nutty doctor's (yours truly) wishes.

He did not pray for the strength to tolerate his parents. He didn't pray to "Get along better with them," in a vague, nondescript way. He was very specific.

"Thank you Lord for choosing the parents you chose for me. You are wise and wonderful, and I will recognize their precious souls at some time when you make my heart ready. I pray they may be lifted up and drawn to you, and receive all of your good blessings."

Two weeks later, he began to see his parents in a different light. Only a month after that, he actually began to enjoy the company of his parents. His Christian Church-family nurtured his soul and his earthly parents nurtured his personality.

I have trained others in Prayer Therapy, to be free from various shackles that bind them, in a release from the captives. Those shackles might be **anger**, **jealousy**, **fear**, **self-hate**, **depression** (sadness), **anxiety**, **obsessiveness**, or **control of others**, etc.

In each case the prescription is the same. Pray as Jesus taught us to pray in the Lord's Prayer, using your own words, beginning with Acknowledgment, moving on to Reverence and so forth. At Petition, formulate your request for release from those emotions that bind you. Prayer Therapy is a specific petition for God to release us from the negatives that hold us captive. Your petition is that God will set you free from the grip that fear, anger, and other negative emotions have on your life.

Complete the prayer in the Prayer Therapy model as outlined. Within the chapters, there are several examples of complete prayers, as well as opportunities for you to put the phrases in your own words.

After you finish your prayer, wait patiently for reassurance that you have been heard by God. He will fill you with the warmth of his presence. Then, live the remainder of the day, as one who believes God has heard your prayer (living by faith). He will answer it in his own time and in his own way.

We often believe a prayer is only answered if we get exactly what we have asked for . . . and immediately, thank you. Live the day, knowing God has heard your prayer. He will answer it in keeping with his plan for us and for mankind, not ours.

How do I know prayer therapy works, beyond what I have read, studied and observed in others? Through his presence in my own life. I have had various forms of arthritis for years, in addition to a heart condition that causes my heart to race for no reason.

About nineteen years ago I went to the University of Chicago for a Rapid CT, a heart test in which the beating heart is photographed—x-rayed at an exceedingly fast speed. The results were: "Assuming the test is valid, you have a 51% blockage in your left coronary artery, 50% in your main coronary artery, and 25% in your anterior coronary artery. Treat the results as if they are accurate." My physician put me on cholesterol reducing medication.

At the same time, the pain in my right leg was getting worse. My knee and hip were both affected. My concern was *how could I rehabilitate my heart with exercise, when I couldn't walk? And, how could I have surgery on my leg if I could not do the exercises that would follow, due to my heart condition?*

I began a daily, prescriptive prayer therapy for myself, seeking release from buried anger and frustration. I also used visual imagery, picturing angels surrounding me, flowing through me, and flying breathtakingly through my coronary arteries, their wings outstretched, reaming out my arteries like a heavenly roto rooter. I prayed the petition prayer, three times a day for three years, praying God would heal my hip so I could attend to the rehabilitation of my heart.

In mid-June of 1999, I learned I needed hip replacement surgery. It was my hip that was making my knee sore. The cartilage in my knee was fine. The hip surgery would help both areas of my leg, since the pain was radiating from my hip down into my knee and lower leg. Still, I was concerned about my heart condition going into surgery. Then, I learned the CT was being done at a center in Sarasota, Florida, where we would be vacationing.

I made an appointment to have another Rapid CT done while we were in Sarasota County, just a few months before my scheduled hip replacement surgery, October 4. By July, I was unable to walk without a cane and Bill had to push me in a wheelchair when we went to Universal Studios in Orlando.

The results of the Rapid CT? Praise the Lord for his miraculous touch! The results revealed no sign of blockage in any of my coronary arteries, not the left or right, not the main, or the anterior. God had answered my prayers, but he had chosen to glorify his own holy name, not mine. He had not healed my hip so I could attend to my heart. He had healed my heart, completely, so I could attend to the rehabilitation of my hip.

When I told a physician at a pre-op session, God had healed my heart and, admittedly, I had also been taking medication for cholesterol, he gave me a dubious glance and said, "If the medication was that good, everyone would be taking it."

He had missed the entire point! Medication had not healed my heart— God had! God had chosen to heal me in his own time and in his manner.

Prayer therapy provided a specific request for release from anger that held me captive; visualizing my prayers being answered (living the day knowing that my prayers were heard), gave me the opportunity to live my faith.

God's holy angels flowing through my coronary arteries, like baptismal waters, cleansed every part.

Does prayer therapy work? Indeed it does! I have experienced the Lord's healing.

In the next chapters, I will describe negative emotions. You may recognize them on your own through my descriptions. Or, perhaps your counselor has identified or diagnosed a negative condition. I imagine your family has.

In Prayer Therapy, if you are caught by more than one negative emotion, pray three times a day for release from just one of the emotions per week: Week I – anger. Week II – fear. Week III – jealousy and so forth.

Sometimes we are unaware of what is bothering us at the root level. We only see the effects of our deeper problems, such as difficulties we may have with co-works, or friends and family. How do we know which emotions have trapped us? Believe it or not, we can focus on the very behaviors or circumstances that confuse us, if we watch for the significant signs that help us to identify our problem.

Certainly, if you are trapped in depression, you may need an anti-depressant medication. Get some guidance in identifying your buried issues. You may want to take this Prayer Therapy book to a session.

For our purposes, we will look at the symptoms of those negative emotions in order to identify them. This is like looking at how children's behavior makes you feel, in order to discover the goals of their behavior. Following a full devotion example, we will look at our prayer attitude and how it impacts our prayer life.

## GOD HAD A DREAM

"God created man in His own image, in the image of God He created him; male and female He created them. God blessed them; and God said to them, "Be fruitful and multiply, and fill the earth, and subdue it; and rule over the fish of the sea and over the birds of the sky and over every living thing that moves on the earth . . . . God saw all that he had made, and it was very good. And there was evening, and there was morning—the sixth day. (Genesis 1: 27-28, 31)

God had a dream and it was you. You sprang from his heart and were born on his breath. You breathe God each time you inhale. And, yet, you are still not satisfied.

"I'm too short, too tall, too fat, too anything." It never ends. Once you have either changed or made peace with the part you believe is flawed, you obsess over another tiny speck of God who lives within you.

Next, you complain that God made a mistake when he placing you in the family into which you were born. Or, God didn't give you the right talent to make you unique enough or rich enough or wise enough for you to be better than others.

God had a dream and it was you. He loves you just the way you are . . . and too much to let you stay that way, as an old poster read. What he wants to prune, is not how we look or who we are or what we have. He wants to rid us of selfishness, anger, ungratefulness, inhospitality, our lack of generosity, and our inability to love totally. That takes a lifetime. Even then, we still won't be "done." Only in those glimmering, fleeting sparks of light, when Christ shines through us, do we have a glimpse of the dream God had of each of us.

I am no physicist, but there is something in quantum physics that says if you drop your keys along the shore line, the essence of your keys will always remain in the water.

Christ walked through the portal of Heaven and, like the keys in the surf, his essence remains on the eye-reader at the entry. That portal stays open for each of us when the light of Christ is read in our eyes, and we walk through the opening created by the Son of God. We, our humanness, have nothing to do with it. We don't have to be perfect, just willing to be pruned and molded and living in the dream God had for us all along—to be a reflection of Him. Let us pray:

"Heavenly Father, you created each one of us from the perfection of your heart. Holy is your name and sanctified is your dream. May I embrace the vision you had of me when you laid the foundation of the world. Wrapped in your love, I get a glimpse of Heaven. I don't have the words to thank you for your son, Jesus, who by his life and death and resurrection created the doorway to Heaven. When he lives in us, the eye-reader at the portal to Eternity recognizes the shepherd's sheep by his light within us. Forgive me when I turn my eyes from your glory and focus on the dirt at my feet, as if I had to find my own way. I ask that you take away my fear of trusting you. Not so any glory may come to me, but that all glory may go to your son, Jesus, my savior and redeemer. Praise to your Holy name. Praise to your precious son. Amen"
Doris
First posted and Copyrighted Doris Gaines Rapp on www.prayertherapyrapp.blogspot.com in 2010

Chapter 2

**Prayer Attention or Prayer Attitude**

I once heard someone say, "I don't pray formally. I am too busy doing God's work. I actually pray all the time, because I am always in an attitude of prayer."

On the one hand, I agree with them. When our heart is turned toward God, we are in a reverent attitude of prayer. But, we are not praying. Jesus was our example of a person who always walked in a prayerful attitude. He was in an attitude of prayer moment by moment. Yet, he set aside time to pray to his father, God. He even took time to give a pointed, step by step tutorial in how to pray, within the context of what we call the Lord's Prayer. If he, who was God incarnate, took time to pray, should we not do the same, even more diligently, more regularly and more earnestly?

When using Prayer Therapy, pray prescriptively, three times daily; in prayer therapy form. Trust me. I know all of the excuses. I have used every one you can think of and probably many more. I certainly don't skip praying because I'm trying to avoid God and I know you don't either. We simply get caught up in the world's demands and we forget. We cannot overcome the world without God, since it is only the Spirit of Christ within us who has overcome the world. Satan has even lured us into neglecting our relationship with God by convincing us that the tasks we have decided to take on are worthwhile, and are of more value than the time we take in prayer. How ridiculous that sounds when we read those words back to ourselves.

*Prayer Therapy of Jesus*  Doris Gaines Rapp, Ph.D.

Everything worth doing is not worth doing now, well, or by us. It is all a matter of priorities. We have each been called to our own ministry. Our ministry certainly includes the rearing of our children. These are the ones we have been called to love, our own children and families. When we go to meet our maker, it will not matter how many non-family members we have led to Christ if we have neglected the ones he gave us to care for and nurture in our own homes.

All others feed our ego. Our family feeds our soul as we nourish theirs.

Quite frankly, it is much easier to make an impression on others, than it is to impress our own family. So, we run out into the world where we can have our ego stroked and where we can be admired by others. However, a truly successful person is one who is admired by their own family, by those who know them best.

We cannot do the awesome task of directing our family to Christ without the constant presence of God. We must be on our knees daily and even then, our children will make their own decisions about their personal walk with Christ.

To ask for our own needs, or in intercession for others, we must be in prayer three times per day. Even then, God will not "perform" for us like our own personal Merlin. God will answer all prayers with positive responses. Those responses will be in keeping with his will. It is our life-task to be in his will and not demand he be in ours.

We must "wait upon the Lord." For many of us, the "wait" will be our ministry—but what a glorious service! To be called to faithfully "wait" is as breathtaking, our "magnificent obsession," as is the call to "go." Both are equal in God's service and both have kingdom building repercussions.

To "go" is to draw attention to oneself. To "wait" is to draw attention to God. While we wait, we use the Secret Prayer of service. If we have done nothing but "wait" at the end of our days, we will have fulfilled our calling and he will say, "Come to me, my good and faithful servant." Could anyone possibly ask for more? To be saved through grace, to live a life of quiet service, is an awesome calling. To live within the love of God, should be enough for anyone.

Max Lucado has said, "You see, from heaven's perspective, grace is enough. If God did nothing more than save us from hell, could anyone complain?" (Lucado, 1996, pg. 131).

Now, let us turn to those conditions that keep us from service, either in "going" or in "waiting," that many of us will recognize. The following sections describe the symptoms of several of the emotional problems many people experience. As you read through them, you may see your own symptoms and behaviors, as well as those of your family and friends. Speak to those you love about seeking help and entering into Prayer Therapy, and follow the same course yourself.

## Chapter 3

**We Begin**

Prayer is the portal to the divine. Do not be afraid to step through. You leave self behind and step into eternity. I don't care how I am used. I would rather be the one who scrapes the mud from others' shoes as they enter into Heaven, than to be locked out at the eternity's door.

Prayer is the key to that doorway. Learning to pray is therefore the "Way"—the path from life to Life. Learning to pray is the purpose of this book, so that Purpose may be found. Once we have learned to pray, we can begin a new life using the Secret Prayer—a prayer for anonymous service.

How do we begin? We are just like Indiana Jones who stepped off into what appeared to be a great abyss, only to discover there was a well-placed but narrow bridge on which to cross. We too must first step out into the unknown, open and available to God, stepping from life into Life. Our Purpose is to be in relationship with God.

Jesus first told the disciples not to pray with the intention of drawing attention to them. We are to pray, focusing on God, and not on who may see us or admire our lofty words.

We identified the phrases of the Lord's Prayer, so we could understand the meaning and then put each line into our own words. The next chapters will venture into the heart of Jesus, by digging beneath the words and entering into a partnership with Jesus in prayer.

## Chapter 4

**Acknowledgment:** *Our Father, who art in heaven.*

Who are we praying to and how do we acknowledge that awareness? God, our father who resides in heaven and in our hearts, is who we are addressing our conversation in prayer. *What God or which god?* You may ask. The God of Abraham, Isaac, Jacob, David, and Daniel: the God and father of our Lord and Savior, Jesus Christ.

We usually don't say, "Yo, God. It's me Gladys." Or, "Hi, ya God, ol' buddy. It's me, Clarence."

You may be asking, did she say, *"Which god?" Are there other gods?* In the twentieth chapter of Genesis, we are told that God gave the Ten Commandments to Moses on the high mountain of Sinai. The tablets of stone were described as having been written with the lightening-bolt finger of God. The third commandment of the ten says, "Thou shall have no other gods before me."

How can we say that there are no other gods if God has said there are? Note how I have written the words "god" and "God." The "other gods," may be other "things" or situations that we honor rather than serving God. "God" with a capital "g" is the name of our heavenly father. He is also called JEHOVAH in the Old Testament.

God is the Life who gave life to everything. He is the creator of all that is created. We do him honor by acknowledging that we are aware he is the one true God above all other gods. And, Jesus taught us even more.

Jehovah God is not only our mighty, all powerful God, he is our father in heaven, or daddy, our "Abba," as Jesus called him.

We think of the strength of a father in several ways. He is powerful, even fearful, like an earth-rattling, ground-breaking earthquake or a lava-belching volcano. That is power—more power than we have ever experienced or witnessed! That is the kind of God, the kind of father that we read about in the Old Testament.

In the New Testament, Jesus showed us that God is more than the creator of laws and admonitions. Jesus taught us about, and reflected, a forgiving, loving father, a daddy who loves to give good things to his children when we lean on him.

When you close your eyes to pray, think of yourself crawling up into the lap of a loving daddy and resting there in his powerful, loving arms. That is the God and Father of the New Testament.

I know that some of you did not have a loving father in your life. I understand that. Some of you have had fathers who yelled, fathers who disappointed you, fathers who were actually mean to you, or even fathers who weren't there at all. Even the most loving father can get tired and cranky sometimes, so no one is perfect. We are not talking about our imperfect, earthly fathers. We're talking about God, our heavenly father who gets it right, perfect, all of the time, not by our demand, but by his design.

Can you possibly imagine someone who never makes a mistake? Someone who is always and forever right?! He is so amazing that, while we are still on earth, we cannot actually gaze on him because our own imperfections would consume us in his perfect presence. And, the perfect God knows you and me personally, and he loves us perfectly. He is our daddy, our Abba.

Perhaps you have heard someone say, "If they really knew me, they wouldn't love me." But, I tell you honestly, God really does know you and me. He even seeks us out, for the simple purpose of loving us. That is the Father in heaven of whom I speak.

*Prayer Therapy of Jesus*  Doris Gaines Rapp, Ph.D.

I remember when I was a child, my daddy would let me comb his hair—part it any way I wanted to, curl it around my finger until it stuck straight up on top then drooped listlessly to the side, like a rooster's red comb. It didn't matter to him. He was there for me. But, my father was far from perfect.

He had a temper that could levitate the roof a good six inches off its true position on the rafters. I am sure some of his choicer words are still hanging over Kettering, Ohio like an echo that has not ceased vibrating to this day. But, I know what a loving father is like, because I choose to remember the nearly perfect love and not the imperfect anger. After all, it is only the love we can take with us into eternity. Why carry around less here on earth?

Our stagnant pain and anger have no place in the hereafter. If I can feel the love from an imperfect earthly father, and remember it with warmth, how much more love can I experience from our heavenly father who loves us perfectly.

"But, Doris," you may say, "I cannot forget my father's anger and violence."

Then I encourage you to make a choice. I challenge you to choose to remember the good and forgive the bad, and if there was no real good, then there was no real father. Perhaps you could remember the love you received from your mother, a grandparent, a minister, a relative or a friend. Choose to remember love, not hate.

When we pray, it is to our heavenly, perfect Father. What picture in our minds can we think of to help us see our father in heaven?

I might picture a five-year-old, strawberry blond, pigtailed little girl with freckles on her nose sitting on her father's lap, parting his hair down the middle until clumps fall on both sides, like dark brown spaghetti spilling over his brow, all the while her father sits patiently humming, slightly off key. For me, that was when time had no actual meaning, and "hurry up," and "keep up" did not exist. That was a time of complete acceptance.

Or, I might picture a young woman in square cap and gown, carrying a diploma across the stage when she graduated with honors. The only person she wanted to see was her seventh-grade educated father popping his vest buttons in pride and love. But, my father died before I earned my doctorate. I like to think he knew, and I know that he would have been proud.

Or, if I really imagine, deeply within my soul, I can see my heavenly father, dressed in glowing white, with perfect love beaming from his eyes, like the brightest sun in a blue June sky, with lightening in his smile, and compassion like thunder in his touch, so loving you almost cannot look at him, standing at the gate to heaven waiting, just for me, to finally come home. That is my heavenly father.

How would you describe your father God, when you close your eyes to pray?

Take your time. Close your eyes and think of several ways in which you might describe your heavenly father. Use happy memories from your past, familiar pictures that make you feel full of love and joy. Then, write them here so that you might refer to them later if you choose to do so.

_____


_____

With a clear picture in mind of God, my father, I am ready to begin my prayer. The first part of my prayer is a verbal acknowledgment that I know to whom I am speaking. I am actually, literally, talking WITH, not to, the God of the universe. Some words I might choose to express that awareness are:

- Oh beautiful loving master . . .
- Our gracious and kind heavenly father . . .
- Great God of all there is . . .
- Abba, Father God . . .

What words might you choose as you acknowledge to whom you are praying? Gather a picture in your mind of the God to whom you are speaking; and, with your picture of God our father in mind, fill in the following space with words of your choice. You might not think of as many as you would like on this first attempt. That's all right. You can go back later and fill in some other descriptive phrases which will help you know to whom you are speaking.

- 

- 

- 

-

## A Quiet Thunder

"He says, 'Be still, and know that I am God; I will be exalted among the nations; I will be exalted in the earth.'" Psalm 46: 10

"Be still . . . ." Is it actually possible, in our time, to *be still?* When I think of all we do, regardless of age: work, school, sports, home, friends, church, hobbies, family and . . . well you get the idea. To know God, we must first *be still*.

You can practice stillness by selecting a favorite Bible verse and meditate or focusing on it for five or ten minutes. When the mind drifts off to the worries or tasks of the day don't be concerned. Brush the thoughts away like a pesky fly and return to the holiness of God's presence in His word. Be still . . .

. . . and know. The verse doesn't say, "I think maybe there must be a God up there—somewhere," or "I wish it were true." It says, ". . . and know . . . that I am God." When we *know* that God is real, when we *know* that He is present, when we *know* that His promises are true, we become filled with His Holy presence. Others may not see the mountains in our life move, or the lightening crack open the sky and let down a golden ladder into Heaven. But, there is a rolling thunder of the soul when the voice of God vibrates within our heart and brings all our melodies into perfect harmony with Him. Be still and know . . . Let us pray:

"Father God, when you speak, your words are like the timpani of a song, the climatic roll of the kettledrum and its quiet beat that provides hope and constant measure, a rhythm to which I move. Holy is your name and precious is your beat of life. I choose this day to be still. I choose this day to know. I choose this day to allow the quiet thunder of your beating heart, to

measure my stride and give me life. Forgive me when I have walked cautiously along your paths. The only true walk is to the drumbeat of your melody, written and composed just for me. I pray that I may know you through the stillness of my lives. In Jesus' name I pray. Amen"
Doris
Posted and Copyrighted Doris Gaines Rapp at www.prayertherapyrapp.blogspot.com on 8-4-14

Chapter 5

**REVERENCE/WORSHIP:** *Hallowed be thy name*

The second component of the Lord's Prayer, Reverence/Worship, includes the word "hallowed." What does "hallowed" mean? Webster's Dictionary gave the following definition:

- To make holy or set apart for holy use
- To respect greatly. Jesus taught his disciples, in the second part of prayer, to worship God our Father, to give him profound reverence and respect.

Many of us, often "pray on the run." We offer a prayer as we wait in line to pay for the latest CD at the music store; as we drive down the street on our way to anywhere except where we have been; and, as we juggle our bundles and packages in the mall. We claim we are right, that prayer-on-the-fly is appropriate because we are "always in an attitude of prayer."

What is an "attitude of prayer?" Is our attitude prayerful when we tap our foot in disgust because the guy in line ahead of us has eighteen items in his cart, when the sign clearly says "**12 Items Only**?" We know how many he has because we counted every one of them. "How dare he?" we fume indignantly to ourselves and to God to whom we have been praying.

Is our attitude prayerful when we glare in our car's rear view mirror at the person who just tried to go around us and who we have just triumphantly cut off?

We may actually have the audacity to say, "Thank you Jesus!" implying, of course, *I won! I'm right because you, Jesus, are on my side! Thank you Lord!*

Are we prayerful when we rush about the mall buying more "stuff" because we think the "stuff" we have is not new enough "stuff." Are we prayerful if we cannot afford the "stuff" we drag up and down the mall halls? With all of our new "stuff" we may even have to claim poverty, saying that we don't have enough money to donate to missions on Sunday morning.

A prayerful attitude is an attitude of worship, not an attitude of *Follow me Lord and I will take you to wonderful places*. An attitude of prayer is *Lead me Lord, even though I do not know where you are taking me. I will wait quietly for your direction, even as my feet follow you.*

An attitude of worship is one of reverence, a consummate immersion in adoration and awe. We worship with an attentive, focused, grateful heart. When we are filled with "awe," we are filled with wonder, even a fear, inspired by our perfect father who loves us completely, deeply, and powerfully. We bow to all that purity because we know we are neither perfect nor pure. We are human.

When we say, "Hallowed be thy name," we enter into worship filled with reverence. We are not equal to God. Because of Jesus, we are equal to everyone else on earth; but we are not equal to God our Father. There is no one God values above us and he does not value us above anyone else.

Some Christians actually believe their church or their family or their group is more valued in God's eyes than another. Some Christians believe their experience of Jesus is more perfect than another's. Some say, "But 'they' could not possible know Jesus as I know Jesus because they did not have the same experience that I had." How sad it is to hear such misperceptions. These people are only harming themselves. They are invalidating another Christian's experience and therefore defaming the body of Christ, the Church of Jesus Christ here on Earth.

I remember a college student I counseled with who was desperately trying to be a better Christian. In fact, he was trying to measure up to the public image his well-known Christian family portrayed. One day, feeling useless and defeated he cried, "But Dr. Rapp, you just don't understand. I come from a high-class Christian family."

I responded, "But, that's not possible. There is no class system in Christianity." Paul said, there is neither male nor female, slave nor free, in the inheritance-line of all God has for the followers of his son, Jesus. In Christianity, we are all equal. But, we are not equal to God. We are not little gods.

When we are in an attitude of worship and reverence of the Lord, we acknowledge that God is so much larger than we are. We could not possibly understand or know all there is to know or experience of God. How could our mighty God be that small? When we demand, "We are close to God and others are not," we are only fulfilling an earthly, self-centered need of our own. We are not in an attitude of worshiping God. When we say "Hallowed be thy name," we bring holiness in our prayer, an attitude of worship and reverence.

Now, as we continue to learn how to pray, I want us to think about words we can use to express Worship, Reverence. First, I will give you some examples.

These are the words I might use from time to time to worship my God.

- I bow before you.
- How magnificent is your love.
- Your peace is comfortable.
- How glorious is your name.
- How splendid is your power and plan.
- Your creation is majestic.

Now it is your turn. Take your time. There is no time limit and there will be no grand prize to the winner or booby prize to the last one to complete their list.

My father used to like to play cards. To the last place winner he would say, "You've just won the crocheted bathrobe," a dubious prize at best, one that just does not quite cover the situation. We are all winners when we learn how to communicate with God.

There is no "second" place or silver medal. There are no "right answers" or "wrong answers." There are just "your answers" and "my answers." All are valuable to God.

There is no blue ribbon for "the most." One expression of worship may be all you need. For learning purposes, I challenge you to write several statements of Reverence so you can learn to express yourself to God in prayer in a variety of ways in order to cut down on the ritualistic repetition of overly used words. So, grab your pencil and begin to write a few words of Reverence and Worship, phase two of our Lord's Prayer, in the space below.

- 
- 
- 
- 
- 
-

## WHAT ARE YOU CALLED?

"He brought Simon to Jesus, who looked at him and said, 'You are Simon son of John. You are to be called Cephas' (which is translated Peter)." John 1:42

Jesus changed Simon's name to Cephas which is Aramaic for Peter. In Greek, Peter means petros, or stone. Remember, later Jesus said, "Upon this rock I will build my church."

Names were very important in the time of Jesus. Their name identified their linage and what others expected of them. In early Europe, a person's surname usually identified their career or job. John Baker was a baker and Mr. Tailor was a tailor. In the case of Simon, Jesus called him his solid rock.

What would Jesus re-name you or me? We have no idea what our future will be and what part we might play in service to God. It is said, "The only predictor of the future, is the past." If you were to choose one word that defines you, what would it be? Is it pleasing to God? Would He have given you that name or is it only a self-serving descriptor?

If I were able to give you a blessing, it would be that you know yourself so well, you can be described in one word, and that word comes from the heart of God, who knows you, even better than you know yourself. Let us pray:

*Prayer Therapy of Jesus*  　　　　　　　　　　Doris Gaines Rapp, Ph.D.

"Name above all names, Glorious Lord, I humbly bow in your presence. Come Sweet Love and let me live in your world and may your Word come alive in me. I ask that you take my life and claim it for your own, renaming me whatever is your will. I would rather be called Sweeper and gather up the crumbs from under your table than to not be included at the Banquet of Joy. Forgive me when I think I must do something great in order to serve you. Every job in the kingdom is equal to the next. While I know that, my earth-bound heart forgets. I love you Lord, call me anything . . . just call me unto yourself. In the name of Jesus Christ, your son and my Lord, I pray. Amen"
Doris
Posted and Copyrighted Doris Gaines Rapp at www.prayertherapyrapp.blogspot.com on 3-6-12

Chapter 6

**Pray for Christ's Return: Thy kingdom come**

Sometimes it is very hard for us to pray for the return of Christ. We want him to return but we feel we need for him to arrange his return around our schedule. We are afraid his return will interfere with our own plans! "Come Lord Jesus . . . but not right now. It's not convenient for me today."

All Christians are to pray for the swift return of Jesus Christ and the ushering in of God's kingdom on earth. Some groups believe they know precisely when he will return. That seems very strange to me. Even Jesus said he did not know when he would return. How presumptuous of us!

Yes, we are called to pray for the return of the Christ. If we try to make it part of each and every one of our prayers, we will not forget to include it in some of our prayers.

What does it mean for Christ to return? He will usher in the day when God, and therefore good, will reign on earth. It will be the completion of God's plan.

It is God's desire that we all pray for his kingdom and his will, not our own.

Think about it. If our plan runs in opposition to God's plan, who do you think will win in that power struggle? And, who in their sane mind would want to win that war—to be against God . . . and win?

What if God actually let us win our own little battles? The amazing thing is, sometimes he does! Have we really won anything of value when we win in a conflict with God? To be in opposition to God is to oppose Love, Truth, Good, Salvation, and Eternal Life.

God has given us rules and laws but we still argue with God over their interpretation. A lie is only a lie in certain circumstances, we argue. A theft is okay when our need is greater than another's right to own. We delude ourselves with many rationalizations.

"But Mom, all the kids are going to the party. Jason's parents trust him. They're letting him go unchaperoned."

This argument is a challenge for teens and for parents. The parents must hold to what they know to be right and in keeping with their values. The teen must yield to their parent's authority when they cannot see the logic behind a parent's decision.

Soon after I got my driver's license, I drove the family car over to the mall, perhaps two miles away. On my way home, I decided to take a little drive in the country. A two mile drive is too short for a newly independent driver. While cruising around the beautiful countryside, listening to music, I started switching radio stations looking for music with a better beat, a brighter sound. As I remember it, I was going pretty fast and was looking down at the radio dial when the road curved and the car didn't. Cars respond to all the basic laws of trajectory. Once set on a certain path, cars will continue on that path even if the underlying support structure (the road) alters direction, unless they are steered to follow a corrected course, which of course involves an attentive driver.

Then it happened! I rattled, bumped, and skidded off the paved road, slammed into a telephone pole, and smashed the passenger side of the car. When I got home, I was still shaking from the "accident" and trembling for fear of what my father would say, since he was prone to angry tirades as I previously shared with you. His only comment, earnestly spoken, was, "What a great lesson you have learned . . . without getting hurt. You cannot drive fast and stay on the road." It was that simple.

*Prayer Therapy of Jesus*  Doris Gaines Rapp, Ph.D.

I was not in line with my father's plan for me, or for his plan for the family car. I knew I was not supposed to drive fast, but I did anyway. Daddy did not control me when I was away from home. I made my own choice. I won, didn't I? Or, did I? Daddy's plan had not changed. He wanted me to keep my eyes on the road and drive at a safe speed. I drove fast, the way I wanted to. That did not make me a winner. I could have lost everything. I only lost my pride and the family car. My dad gained another opportunity to show that he was right and that he was a loving, forgiving father.

In our prayer time we do not have to pray for the completion of God's plan and the second coming of Christ. That will not stop his plan, however. It will only put us in opposition to God's will. That is not a good position from which to honker down and fight. I do not believe we will ever win an argument with God. An argument won, is a life lost. Do you really believe you can turn your back on God's plan and still be fulfilled, still happy? We are to pray daily, for the second coming of Christ and the beginning of his kingdom on earth.

As I was thinking about a variety of ways in which I might pray for God's kingdom to come, I developed these phrases:

- May your kingdom come on Earth.
- May the time of Christ's return be swift.
- I know not when you are to come, but I am thankful you know.
- It is not necessary for me to know when you are coming—you do.
- I pray for your kingdom to rule in my heart until you return.
- I give up all my plans, to make room for your kingdom now.

Now, it is your turn. You are to put your thoughts about Christ's coming again, for God's kingdom to reign, into your own words. Take your time and let the real meaning of *Thy Kingdom come* travel all the way to your heart.

There is no rush. Write down your own words as I have done.

-

- 

- 

- 

- 

- 

As we wait for his return, we pray that our lives can be in harmony with his plan. We pray for his return, and yet his church is already here. Sometimes, the children of God within Christ's church bicker and claim they are the most loved. Sometimes, we measure the "success" of Jesus Christ and his church by numbers.

## FULL BY EXTENSION

"For where two or three come together in my name, there am I with them." (Matthew 18: 20 (NIV ©1984)

"The biggest is best." We apply that statement, right or wrong, to everything, even to churches. The mega-church does have some great features:

• Small groups where Christian relationships are formed
• A variety of activities, some of which may interest you

A small church has:

• A small group where Christian friendships are born and that is why you attend
• Activities where your talents are of service

Maybe every pew is not filled in the little church you attend. Remember, beloved of God, every time a child puts on warm mittens or a bright cap through a mission of your church, that child sits with you in church. Every time a marathon runner eats a bowl of warm soup from the outreach of your members, that athlete is there on the pew with you and takes your love with them wherever they go. Every time an inmate from your jail ministry turns his heart from himself and focuses his prayers on the needs of his/her family, he and that entire family join in Christian praise and fellowship in your little church each Sunday morning. Your church is full— through the extension of your love and outreach.

Praise the Lord, not for large numbers, but for large hearts. Praise him not for glittering gold church adornments, but for the sparkle in a child's eyes or the love in a shut-in's heart. The church of Jesus Christ, in worship of the Lord God, is not contained within any church building or crammed into the balcony. The church is on the streets, in the homes, workplaces, and agencies where the members carry his word, hope, and grace. Every church is full by an extension of each member's love. Let us pray:

"Father of every one of us, whether we worship in large groups or small, you are always there within our midst when we gather in your name. I praise your holiness. May I dwell within your presence, even after I leave your sanctuary, for your work is done beyond the building's walls. Your first-kingdom has come, in the worship, love and presence of Christ's church. May none of your children boast of being more blessed than another by virtue of size or wealth or opportunity. I know you choose to bless your children with the work to which you have called each of us. May today be the day when I look beyond the sanctuary walls and seek to expand your love in new and less familiar places. I know I will not walk alone out there. You will go with me and cover me with your own presence. The great cloud of witnesses that have gone before, and those who pray for me, and each of us, from the church pews, will uphold me with their prayers. Forgive me when I thought your ministry was only for those within the church's walls. While it begins there, it flows through the streets of my town and further outreach, when I am willing to be a conduit and not a funnel. Give me courage and strength to carry your love and grace where the church doors end, and your greater world begins. In the name of Jesus, your son and our redeemer I pray. Amen"
Doris
First posted and copyright on www.prayertherapyrapp.blogspot.com on 2-4-13

## Chapter 7

**Surrender:** *Thy will be done in earth as it is in heaven.*

I heard someone tell a friend, "When you pray for healing, don't even ask God if your request is God's will, because you already know it is his will."

In other words, whatever you want, God will supply it because what you want is always within God's will for you. How arrogant! Is God, our heavenly Father, a follower of ours or are we disciples and followers of Jesus Christ, God's son? Who follows whom? A student, a disciple, a follower, completely yields his/her will over to his/her Master. We give in to God!

If you took a job flipping burgers or heading up the Red Cross, whatever your career choice, you would have to yield yourself to your employer's goals and plans for his/her business. You would not go into the fast food manager and say, "I have a great idea. I'm going to sell golf clubs instead of burgers. Since I knew that you would agree this is a great idea, I didn't even ask your permission. Five crates of clubs will be delivered this afternoon."

Bye! You're out the door.

When we enter into another's employee, or when we follow Jesus as our Master, we take on their plans, their goals, and discard our own. That is the point of "following" another.

When Jesus taught his disciples to pray, he included a statement of surrender.

"Thy will be done in (on) earth as it is in heaven." Wow! Did you hear what you just read? You are praying that his will may be completed in your life as perfectly as it is in heaven. That is total surrender!

Again, we must watch our attitude. We cannot claim to love God and follow his son, Jesus, while we harbor resentment for another; while we have discord with our parents or in-laws; while we claim we know better about someone's relationship with Christ than Jesus does. We can no longer claim another's experience of Christ is invalid or inferior if it is not identical to ours. When we follow, we keep our eyes fixed on Jesus, not on someone else. Jesus will do his work in another's heart. We only assist Him.

We cannot lead someone to Christ when we claim superiority over them. What we are offering is a savior who includes everyone equally. We defame the body of Christ when we put down another's ministry or experience of Jesus.

What does it mean to defame the body of Christ? The followers of Jesus make up his body, his hands, and his feet here on earth. When we say, "So-and-so isn't really a Christian because s/he did not go to the same camp I did or have the same experience I had."

Or, "He doesn't go to the same church I go to; so, he cannot possibly be sincere in his Christian walk."

Some say, "She doesn't give as much, or do as much as I do, so she cannot possibly be in as high a favor with Jesus as I am."

Have you heard, "I joined the group two years ago, when did you join?" You know full well the other person joined the church or group before you did, implying "I came first; therefore, I am more holy than you."

These impressions and statements only turn others away from Christ. Someone seeking a church family can easily see the hypocrisy of the other's claims. We are actually harming, telling lies against (defaming) other followers of Jesus Christ. We are "defaming the body of Christ."

I heard a pastor give the following example in a Sunday sermon. A new Christian from an Evangelical Church in Europe visited a main line church while touring in the United States. He bragged to the pastor of the church about the wonderful programs at his new, independent church in Europe. He gave a testimony of superiority over the main line church because his church had newer, more progressive ideas and was therefore more blessed by God. The pastor smiled and responded gently, "But you must remember, we are the church who kept the flame alive so you could discover it."

We are all needed. We are all valued. We all have different talents and responsibilities. We are all blessed by God when our minds are stayed on him.

We must surrender everything, including our ego, our self-centeredness and self-praise, our own goals and plans, and yield ourselves to God's plan for the world. Our goal becomes, helping to bring about his kingdom on earth, not our interpretation of his kingdom.

Surrender! Wow! Surrender is not really part of the human condition. We are wired to fight for life. God made us that way so that we would be equipped to endure our experience here on earth when things get tough. It is not an automatic reaction to his calling. It is a glorious gift that we give to God, yielding our will over to his.

I remember counseling with a young Christian couple who had made a decision to place the husband at the head of the family. It is not important here whether you agree with that type of family hierarchy. It serves here as an example.

In their interpretation of family, the husband would make all of the decisions, because God had made him "wiser." Therefore, the husband dominated his wife rather than lead by service, as the Bible instructs. I made it clear that his wife had not yielded her power over to him because she was required to. This is the twenty-first century. Every civil court in the country would support her rights as an individual. She yielded her power over to her husband as a gift, a magnificent, awesome present to the husband she loved and the Lord she worshiped and followed. Her husband had a grave responsibility, to treat his wife's gift with honor and respect. She had surrendered willingly.

As we think about surrendering our will to God's and how we might phrase it in prayer, I will give you a few suggestions as I have done above. Just remember, if you surrender your will to God and then constantly take it back, you are having a power struggle with **GOD!** Guess who will win that battle in the long run!

Look at my first surrender statement, "Take my will and mold it to your will." If I try to take that back every day and demand God do things my way, I will be creating for myself a very, very unhappy, energy draining, depressing life.

If I do not want to follow Jesus, God gives me self-will to make that choice. But, if I give my will over to him and snatch it back every day, I am only hurting and exhausting myself. Let it go! My life will be far more perfect in God's hands than it could ever be under my own control!

As you read these statements, remember, you know what is the most difficult for you to surrender better than I. So my suggestions are just that, suggestions. You create statements of surrender for yourself in the space that follows mine. Suggestions:

- Please Father, take my will and mold it to your will.
- I can only surrender my life. May your will begin in me.
- May your will come swiftly to Earth.
- May your will in heaven be duplicated on Earth.
- May I give over my will to your will just as it is completed in Heaven.

Now it is your turn. I know from my own experience, it can be hard to surrender. No one can be more stubborn than I. My family reminds me of that from time to time. As I explained, I prayed for many years, "Father I do not want to surrender, but I want to want to with all my heart." After a period of time, I became aware that my own prayer had taken on a life of its own as I began to pray, "Lord, I want to surrender to you."

I frequently suggest to clients in therapy, begin with an "I want to want prayer." I propose they to begin with,

- "Father, I am stubborn. I do not want to surrender to you, but I really want to want to." You may choose to make your first prayer, a prayer of "I want to want to . . ."
- "Dear Loving Lord, I give my life freely to you."

Now, you begin:

-

-

-

-

-

## FLASH! BANG!

"Thou wilt keep *him* in perfect peace, *whose* mind *is* stayed *on thee*: because he trusteth in thee." (Isaiah 26:3 KJV)

"I've been hit!" My thoughts raced as I drove down I-69 on Saturday afternoon in a welcomed down pour. I was on my way home from a Christian Women's meeting and felt blessed. Dark clouds had been gathering overhead all day, then the rain hit, fast . . . blinding. Then, it happened. There was a quick, blinding flash outside the car beside me and a simultaneous BANG, followed instantly by a quick "sizz" sound up the driver's side of the car and window. I knew immediately. I had been struck by lightning!

At home, I jumped out of the car and searched the door and side panels for any evidence of the strike. I saw nothing unusual. I was thankful I had just gotten new tires a few weeks ago. There had been plenty of rubber between me and the bolt from the sky.

God had really blessed me that day. I had attended an inspirational meeting in the morning and early afternoon, followed by a safe and leisurely drive home, in spite of the electricity in the air. Just like the rubber grounded me safely to the pavement, God had grounded me safely to Him as well.

Do we make sure our spiritual tires are refreshed each day? Is there a thick layer of prayer-power between us and the world? Is the air we breathe, like the thoughts we entertain, pure and holy unto God? We live in a world of thunder bolts and lightening jolts. When we give our will over to God, we ride above the road, in the safe peaceful embrace of His grace and love. Let us pray:

*Prayer Therapy of Jesus*                    Doris Gaines Rapp, Ph.D.

"Father God, I hold your name in reverence. For I know, when I call upon your name, blessings rain down on those I name. You are more awesome than I can ever imagine and your name has more power than I will ever know. I take this moment today to thank you for all the blessings you have bestowed on me, the protection you have given to me and my loved ones, and the blessed fellowship you have so generously given. Forgive me when I have withheld my will and believed that peace is something I can work toward or acquire on my own. Peace comes when I surrender and find my rest in you. In your loving arms, I am protected from the dangers around me. I am not childish enough to believe that bad things will not happen to those who love you. I thank you that you protect my soul from the evil one at all times, until you bring me safely home to you. For all of these blessings, I thank you, and pray for continued rest in the hollow of your hand. In the precious name of Jesus Christ, our savior, I pray. Amen"
Doris
Posted and Copyrighted Doris Gaines Rapp at www.prayertherapyrapp.blogspot.com on 9-26-11

## Chapter 7

**Petition:** *Give us this day our daily bread.*

We are not to pray for the newest computer or the fastest car; not a bigger house or the flashiest clothes; not to attain riches or fame. "Daily bread" is any basic need that is necessary for the current day—worship, shelter, food, relationships, clothing, release from ills. Today is the only "real" there is. What is past is gone; what is coming is maybe; but what is now, is real, and today is as real as it gets. We are to pray for what is real. Someone said, "God will supply our needs, not our wants."

"Daily bread" can also be the love, acceptance, and relationship only God can give. Each day, we need a new commitment to live in his will and love.

Each day, we invite him to supply our spiritual nurturance. Each day, we ask to be spiritually fed by him.

Prayers of Petition can be for other people, our country and our world. When we petition God, we request something of him. Our prayers of petition are our opportunity to go to God as our father, our Abba, and ask his blessing, his healing, his goodness, for ourselves and for others.

My own prayers of petition have matured over the years as I matured in my relationship with God. I was fifteen years old when the Pilot Mission for *Youth Mission to Youth* came to the Evangelical United Brethren churches in the Dayton, Ohio area. College youth from all over the country converged on the Dayton of my youth and helped to ignite my spiritual flame and captured my imagination.

*Prayer Therapy of Jesus*  Doris Gaines Rapp, Ph.D.

The following summer, my older sister, Donna, was selected to participate on the eastern team of Youth Mission to Youth while I waited at home. Her letters home were full of the work the Holy Spirit was doing in the lives of the Missioners and the local youth they served.

During the following fall and winter, I prayed to God daily and I lobbied Dr. John Knecht, the Assistant Secretary of Evangelism for the Evangelical United Brethren General Offices located in Dayton, at every opportunity. I knew I would be one of the youngest; I was only sixteen but would be seventeen by summer. I wanted to be a Youth Missioner more than anything I had ever prayed for up to that time in my young life. Finally, in the spring, I received my acceptance letter.

The Mid-West Youth Mission to Youth team traveled from Ohio to the Dakotas during the next summer. It was one of those rare experiences in life by which we actually mark time—my life before Youth Mission to Youth and all of my life after Youth Mission. How could one ever describe the experience: for six weeks, we lived together, ate, traveled, laughed, studied, and prayed with a close knit group of like-minded young adults, and two or three of us who were teenagers? We spent long sessions in prayer. We evangelized personally, giving our testimonies on a one-on-one basis and in massive groups at the weekend's evangelistic service. Hundreds of youth pressed to get near the alter; some could only kneel in the aisles and at their seats in the pews, as they accepted Christ as their personal savior. We became a group that breathed as one soul all in synchrony with God's will and loving presence.

We oriented ourselves to the work ahead of us at Indiana Central College, now the University of Indianapolis. I was unsure of myself. Everyone seemed so much more centered in Christ, more mature, more confident. But, I pressed on, since the ministry in front of me was far more compelling and captivating than my fears.

We spent a week in each of the six cities in as many states, praying with and nurturing the youth in collective seminars. In the evenings, we lived and worked with two or three missioners in the local churches. Days were spent in training the local youth to evangelize in their neighborhoods. We sang wonderful choruses of praise and glory. We laughed at creative skits and enjoyed fun loving friends. We prayed as one heart, longing to be of service to our Lord, in praise and intercession for each other and the community.

Sometime, half way through the first week in the first mission area, I remember praying, "God, you know me. I'm not sure what I am doing here or how I can serve you but please use me anyway, in spite of myself." And, God answered my prayer and the collective prayers of the missioners. Many souls were won to Christ through the mighty wind of the Holy Spirit that blew through the churches and hamburger joints along the way through the communities of Central United States.

I remember one young man who sat on a small hill that rose a few feet above the three or four hundred other youth who had gathered for the first night's "mixer" in one Ohio town. He was about twenty-one or twenty-two and to me, at seventeen, that was very old. It wasn't so much that he just sat there, hands folded across his knees, it was the look on his face—a look of pain and loneliness that captured my attention. I have always loved a challenge, so I began to talk with him, as reticent as he was.

"Come on and join the group," I began.

But he said, "No thanks" and little more.

I whispered a prayer for God's help so I would say the right thing. I sat beside the sad soul who presented such a contrast to the happy faces in the group on that summer evening. Out of my own inexperience and God's perfection the boy/man began to unveil his story like layers of tissue being peeled away from a precious but hidden secret treasure.

"I'm Bobby," he began when he felt comfortable and safe. Maybe he opened up when he sensed my immaturity yet genuine interest in him. "I'm Bobby and I just got out of prison for killing my best friend in a car accident."

Once the barred gate was opened, the grief he had been experiencing poured from his lips and dissipated into the mist and the evening dew. Bobby talked quietly until he had said it all, the regret, the humiliation, the grief and pain.

Finally, I was able to help Bobby to his feet so he could join some of his friends who had come to participate in the fun.

Later, the minister of his church said that Bobby had not talked about the accident since he got out of prison and marveled that I was able to get him to open up. How did I do it? Believe me, I did nothing. I would not have known how if I had tried. But, I did pray a simple prayer of petition for help in ministering to the young man in order to meet his needs and not my own. I asked God to work his miracle of love through me and then I got out of the way, so the Lord could work.

As you see, our petitions must be specific—like, today's "bread" or specific "words." Later, we will talk more about Prayer Therapy, one of the parts of prayer not included in the Lord's Prayer. Note that Prayer Therapy is a form of petition prayer and is requested at this point in our pray. For now, let us just learn to be very specific in our praying, which is essential for petitions.

For examples of specific petitions, prayed on the real, daily, present level, I have written the following petitions. Some are petitions for others. Some are personal requests. As I was writing them, I realized how hard it is for me to ask God for anything even now. I feel I should be giving to him. But, Jesus not only condoned petitioning in prayer, he taught his disciples to include petitions in their own prayers. Examples:

- Father, please give me water to quench a thirst only you can satisfy.
- Father, please give me a listening friend today. I have a lot to say.
- Father, my dear friend (name) is so angry, please release him from the power that anger holds over his life and wrap him in your love and peace. I acknowledge my own anger as well. Please release me also from anger's grip like a mighty vice and set me free from its grasp.
- Please clear my head so I can sleep well tonight and answer questions clearly tomorrow.

*Prayer Therapy of Jesus*                    Doris Gaines Rapp, Ph.D.


- Oh Father, I need $12.89 today to buy a book my daughter needs.
- Please help me to see any opportunity to earn that amount or to accept it as impossible if it is not your will.
- Please help me to be thankful for all I have, no matter what it is.
- Father, (name) has cancer and needs your healing. Release him/her from the power of fear so s/he may be healed in body and soul and set him/her free to accept your will for his/her life.

I know how hard it is to ask others for anything. Still, that is what we are invited to do. We are to go to God and ask him for the very specific thing we need today.

First, we have to know what we need. Take some time to think about your needs—not your wants and desires. What is a necessity for today? First of all, you need God in your life each day. Think of a way to express that. Then, ponder other basic bread-of-life-things you need and write them down.

- 

- 

- 

- 

- 

-

## WRITTEN ON HIS HANDS

"See, I have written your name on the palms of my hands. Always in my mind is a picture of Jerusalem's walls in ruins." (Isaiah 49: 16 New Living Translation)

God will never forget his children. Isaiah spoke of his love for Israel and even while it stood in rubble, he remembered every name. The marvelous parallel is Jesus our Savior; he will never forget us. Our names are written in the wounds on the palms of his hands.

I have received several prayer requests in the last few days: physical and mental illness, death, feelings of abandonment and as many more as there are those who are in pain. God will bring healing to his children, in his time and within his plan.

We hear the dreaded news from our physician and pray that we will be healed. We stand beside the bed of our dying loved one and pray for recovery, only to have him/her slip away. We see our children exercise their independence, the very thing we have trained them to do during all their years of growing up in our home, but feel rejected when they leave. My precious friends, God has your name, and the name of your loved one, written in blood on the hands of his own Son. There is absolutely no way he will let them slip through his fingers, untouched by his love and grace.

Healing will come: healing of body, healing of relationships, and healing of the pain that follows the death of someone close. It can do no less. Jesus Christ reaches out his pierced hands and blesses us and others, every time we call on him. Let us pray:

"Father, God, I recognize your holy presence all around me. I ask that your perfect will be done in my life and the lives of those I love. Heaven is full of those who went before us, making wide the way first opened by your son, Jesus. May Heaven come near and set up your kingdom in my life as I surrender my desires and plans to you. For this day, I ask for your healing hand on my body and on those I name. Take away any fear and anger and anxiety that accompany the illnesses we have. I know that the negative emotions contribute to the weakening of the body. Free me from my desire to control whom you will heal and in what manner. Release me from my need to tell you about a better plan for me and my loved ones, than your perfect plan. I thank you that power and glory are yours alone. I pray all these things in the name of Jesus, in whose palms my name, and the names of all those I have lifted up in prayer, are written. Amen"
Doris

Posted and Copyrighted Doris Gaines Rapp at www.prayertherapyrapp.blogspot.com on 9-22-14

## Chapter 8

**Pray For Forgiveness:** *And forgive us our debts (trespasses) as we forgive our debtors (those who trespass against us).*

We can sometimes get into such a habit, as we pray the Lord's Prayer that a cadence begins to sounds as if we were marking off time on a metronome. But, the prayer of our Lord is not simple prose with any real meaning. Jesus said we are "to pray in this manner." Certainly, he would not have told us to pray in a style God would not honor or to which he would not respond. So, think for a moment about what you just prayed.

Loosely interpreted, "and forgive us our debts (trespasses) as we forgive our debtors (those who trespass against us)" means: *Father, forgive me to the same degree and in the same manner I forgive others.* That is what we have prayed all of our lives! Look more closely at what we were really asking when we prayed to be forgiven in the same manner we forgive others.

- "I forgive my brother about half the time, so God forgive me approximately half of the time, also."

- "Father, I tell people I forgive them in order to make myself look good, but I'll really harbor anger and resentment against them forever. I'll never trust them again. Father God, tell me you forgive me too, so I will believe you are forgiving me, but it's okay to remind me of my sin every time we talk. I understand you will never trust me again."

If God forgave me to the degree and in the same manner in which I have forgiven others, I would never be set free from my sins. He would always qualify his forgiveness and give it away only to take it back later.

Forgiveness is a gift from God, part of that whole package called "Grace." We certainly have not earned it or deserve it. We need to put others into the same position we are in. They have not earned our forgiveness simply because they ask to be forgiven. And, perhaps they do not deserve our forgiveness due to the gravity of their misdeeds. But, we are still called to be forgiving. God forgives. We are called to be forgiving, to take on the nature of God, as one of his children, as we are forgiving to others.

Let us not forget the complete process. Remember what we are to do. **Go** and make restitution and **then** take our petitions before God. Most of us would like to omit the first step, going to the one we have offended. We would like to save ourselves from the embarrassment of apologizing or repairing a damaged relationship. We would prefer going to God in secret, claim the promise of his forgiveness and forgo the restitution to another. In that way, no one else would know of our transgression. We could still come off looking as perfect as we try to pretend we are.

I have counseled with clients who have come from very well-known Christian families. These young adults have come into my office furious about their family life. What Dad claimed in his newest book or in the pulpit on Sunday morning regarding the role of the father as the head of the house, is not lived out behind the closed doors of their home. Dad sits in front of the TV and doesn't get involved with the children, while Mother makes all of the decisions each day. Let us not become too critical of them, however. We do the same, or a similar kind of deceiving.

We want to be forgiven without admitting we have sinned (or aren't perfect as we have claimed). Forgiveness can only come when we go to those we have offended and admit our wrong doings, make restitution, and ask for forgiveness.

Restitution must come first. We cannot just say, "I'm sorry." *I'm sorry* really doesn't solve anything. We have to correct our mistakes. We can admit our sins to God and ask for his strength in making it right, then follow through with our commitment to make restitution. Forgiveness can then take place.

According to Louis Smeads (1984), the last stage of forgiveness is the reconciliation we make after forgiveness. Reconciliation means that the one who has offended must have the capacity to feel the pain that s/he has inflicted on the other and make things right with them. After I have gone to the one I have offended, I can take my petitions for forgiveness before God.

As I pray for my own forgiveness, I may need to be vague and specific at the same time. I need to ask for forgiveness for things I did which I didn't even know that I had done, as well as for things I know I had done.

When I was an elementary school child, my mother told me to change my dress every day after school to save it for the next day. However, if the dress was very soiled, I could keep it on as I played after school in the house or in the wonderful half-acre yard around our home. One day after school, my mother called me in from play to put on "everyday clothes." My responses was, "What's wrong Momma, didn't I get it dirty enough?"

Sometimes we know very well how "dirty" our lives have become because of our deliberate actions. Other times, we acknowledge we are not perfect and we realize we probably hurt someone when we were not even aware of it.

We are harder on ourselves than on anyone else. We do not consider ourselves worthy of forgiveness. Well, truthfully, we aren't. But we don't ask for forgiveness on our own merits—what we have done to compensate for our misdoings, or how many good deeds we have done. We ask for forgiveness because Jesus is worthy. We pray in his name and with his power. When we pray daily for forgiveness, in the present moment, we begin to understand realness.

As I pray for forgiveness, I will need to be forgiven for what I know I did. I also acknowledge my imperfections. The forgiveness section of my prayer may be something like this:

- Father, I owe so many people for kindnesses. Forgive me for being unkind to (name). I will ask for their forgiveness, too.
- I know I have not perfectly forgiven (name). Help me to better forgive him/her. Please forgive me for the wrongs I have done to others, even when I have not been aware of them.
- Father, forgive me more each day as I learn to forgive (name). Father, I really do not feel like forgiving (name) but I earnestly want to feel like forgiving him/her. May only your perfect forgiveness shine through me when I see him/her, and not my imperfection.

I know it is very hard for many of us to admit our weaknesses. But, our Father already knows our limitations and imperfections. He already knows how we struggle to be kind to an obnoxious boss, fellow student, or co-worker. He knows when we have hurt someone or when we have turned our back on the Lord himself to follow the world. And, he will forgive us. We need only ask him.

The following space is for you to express yourself to God and ask him for forgiveness. You don't have to share what you have written with anyone. On the other hand, you may want to reveal the areas in which you struggle in order to illicit help from a friend. They can help you stay on task as you learn to forgive and hold you accountable. You may even want to seek professional therapy or counseling as you learn to forgive. Until you can forgive others, you will not be free to forgive yourself or find happiness and freedom from depression.

Whatever you write here can be changed or added to later. You can also go back and mark your progress in forgiveness as you mature enough to forgive others.

- 
- 
-

## GOD BLESS OUR NATION

"If my people, who are called by my name, will humble themselves and pray and seek my face and turn from their wicked ways, then will I hear from heaven and will forgive their sin and will heal their land." 2 Chronicles 7:14 NIV ©1984

In the United States, we celebrate Flag Day each year in June. To my readers in other countries, "Do you set aside a day to recognize what your flag means to you?"

Our flag represents Freedom to us. Your flag may represent loyalty, bravery, and/or love of country. Whatever the words behind our banners, may today be the day that those words are forever linked to God the Creator.

May our LOYALTY be to God, the author of Life and Love; our BRAVERY, the courage to speak truth to those around us and testify to the blessings from God in our lives. May our LOVE OF COUNTRY be an acknowledgment that the Lord God of Love and Peace is the ultimate authority over our people. Where FREEDOM is represented by our flag, we lift up the name of the one true God and thank him for the blessing of Freedom he has given us.

We are all his children, across the entire expanse of his creation. May the banner that flies over all of us represent Loyalty, Bravery, Love of Country, and the Freedom he has given to all his children who will humble themselves before him, and acknowledge his sovereignty over our lives. We must first seek forgiveness for our thoughts of superiority and admit, with humility, that the only Glory there is belongs to God, the Father of us all. Let us pray:

"Holy Father, Abba, Daddy to all of your children who bend their knee to you, I lift up your name in praise. May your kingdom unfold to all of your people, wherever they may be. I ask that Love and Peace flow from you and fill my life to overflowing. Where there is no Love, the people parish from the inside out. Where there is no peace, your children destroy themselves. Where loyalty does not reside, your children follow false gods. Where no bravery abides, your children live in fear and do not receive the blessings of the testifier. Where there is no love of country, your children sell their country short and do not lift up what it offers the people of the world. Without freedom, no one is free. May I realize that freedom comes to those who are willing to stand up and to live as the free people we were created to be. Forgive me for my lazy faith and my apathetic ways, because my indifference will cause our freedoms to erode and disappear. May today be the day I accept my responsibility, to carry on the Freedoms you have given me. May I be loyal to you and brave when my freedoms are attacked. Let my love of country shine like the promise it represents. In the name of Jesus, my redeemer, I pray. Amen"
Doris

Posted and Copyrighted Doris Gaines Rapp at www.prayertherapyrapp.blogspot.com on 6-11-12.

Chapter 9

**Deliver Us From Our Sins.**
***And lead us not into temptation but deliver us from evil.***

Our request, to be led away from temptation to sin, is linked to our daily request to be forgiven for our sins as we did when we prayed, ***forgive us our trespasses (debts)***. We plead for forgiveness for what we have already done, *our trespasses*. And, God does forgive us. But, we are human and continue to make mistakes that offend God. Perhaps because we know that we sin daily, many people don't forgive themselves to the generous degree that they forgive others, or in the way God forgives them. Our act of asking for forgiveness can be a daily self-reminder to forgive ourselves.

In the "freedom from temptation" part of the prayer, we ask God to help us not even be tempted to do wrong and to deliver us from the possibility of our yielding to any temptation. I sometimes wonder why we even have to ask God to lead us away from temptation.

Why would he lead us to the edge of temptation when he knows how weak we are? Because he loves us. When we follow Jesus, it is because we choose to do so. Love that has no option but to love is not really love. He allows us to choose sin, so that we can also choose **not** to sin. With God's help, we can make right choices.

Where he leads, we follow, if we are his. When we follow him, we are made safe from "the evil one." The ***deliver us from evil*** part of the prayer is our opportunity to admit that we are weak and we do yield to temptation. When we give in to sin, we open the door to "the evil one."

In the twenty-first century many Christians do not believe there is a Satan or his domain, Hell. And yet, many others are being drawn into satanic worship, witchcraft, and other forms of magic. They certainly believe in the evil one. My message is to them as well. Satan brings death. Jesus Christ brings life. "Lord, lead us not into temptation, but deliver us from evil."

Evil is around us as much now, or maybe more, than it has ever been. The more educated we become, the more devious and deceiving Satan has become. Rather than appearing to mankind as a slithering snake in a pristine garden, Satan crawls in our modern homes through the hypnotic click of the addictive keyboard, the slowly social-shaping shimmer of the television, and even the seemingly innocent little, ugly, monster-shaped toy in your child's cereal box.

These examples of evil are as few as three grains of sand scattered among all the other glittering granules on a warm, inviting beach, luring us into sin. Only God can deliver us from sin and the temptation to sin that is all around us. It presents itself in too many ways and comes at us from all directions. We would be helpless to be on guard every moment from every angle, on our own. In fact, hyper-vigilance would only render us profoundly anxious and paranoid. No place is safe and no one is trustworthy. If we put our trust in God to deliver us from sin and evil, we can rest in the assurance that God is faithful to those who love him. "Lead us not into temptation but deliver us from evil, oh Lord we pray."

We ask God to shield us from the temptation that is all around us and deliver us safely on the other side. We may ask him to shield our eyes from sinful possibilities and deliver us from their power to claim our interest.

Our relationship to God is made stronger as we depend on him to deliver us from temptation. A child is bonded to his or her primary caretaker because the child depends on them for their basic needs and nurturance. Their relationship is made stronger by the child's dependence on his/her parent. We depend on God to deliver us from temptation and our faith is made stronger by our dependence on him.

How might I write this? I have chosen these words.

• Oh Father, I am so easily drawn to overspending (a specific temptation). Shield my eyes from all the pretty "things" I will see in the mall today, and direct my attention to my daughter's blue jeans until you safely deliver me out the door and back to my car.

• Oh Father, I am so tempted to eat a banana split this evening and I know I shouldn't. Please, may I not even be tempted and deliver me safely through the evening, out of temptation's pull.

• An unmarried woman may pray, "I know I am tempted to get too close to my friend's boyfriend. May I remember our friendship and not be tempted to get too close to him."

These suggestions give you an opportunity to see some possibilities as you write your requests for deliverance from temptation and evil.

•

•

•

•

### "Oyez, Oyez, Oyez!"

"The LORD will keep you from all harm—he will watch over your life. The LORD will guard your going out and your coming in, from this time forth and forever." Psalm 121: 7-8 NIV

"Hear ye, hear ye, hear ye," the town crier would call out the news and proclamations of the day. It was against the law to heckle or deter the crier, as they were representative of the crown. Who sits on your throne? Do you hear the messages of the crier who speaks for your king?

A life wasted is one that has been lived serving the wrong monarch. A life squandered is one spent listening to a false crier, an impostor, a perverter of the truth. He dresses in the same red and gold robe, white breeches and black boots as the representative of the King. He looks normal and speaks the words we want to hear. So, we choose to believe him. He represents a god we have created and his words are comfortable. But, it is still a lie.

And still he calls, "Hear ye, hear ye, hear ye, the people of God." But, they would not. Will you be part of the generation that turns from false gods, seeks the truth, and returns to the Lord our God? Let us pray:

"Holy Father, Truth divine, let me hear with this heart of mine. Flood my thoughts with your love and grace, and fill my life with your sweet embrace. Give me your words, both true and pure, to heal my wounds, my stain to cure. Forgive my bent for seeking ease; meet me there upon my knees. Give me a heart that hears your voice, and filters out the whole world's noise. Love divine, oh greater still, the joy of life within your will. Oyez, Oyez, Oyez. Amen"
Doris
Posted and Copyrighted Doris Gaines Rapp on www.prayertherapyrapp.blogspot.com on 9-19-10

## Chapter 10

**Honor God's Omnipresence:** *For thine is the kingdom . . .*

In the King James Version of the Bible, Jesus is recorded as saying we are to honor or recognize God's omnipresence—the recognition that God is everywhere.

And in reverse, everywhere is God's. Are we going to say, "Well, I don't read that in the NIV, so I don't have to include it in my prayer?" They may argue, "All collies are dogs, so all dogs are collies is silly." That may be, but God is not our lap dog.

Aren't we really kidding ourselves when we try to take short cuts, when we attempt to leave God out of part of our lives? Everything we have is God's and everywhere we are is his own back yard as well. "For thine is the kingdom . . ." might be interpreted in three ways.

- Father, everything, in all the kingdom, (the world) is really yours.
- Everything in my world (kingdom) belongs to you, Father.
- You are king of the heavenly kingdom and I honor your sovereignty. [We have to be careful, we are not implying, "You are king in heaven and I am master of my domain on earth."]

If we are God's children, if we are disciples of Jesus Christ, then our kingdom is God's kingdom; God's kingdom is our inheritance; and God is the sovereign king over all.

We usually are more concerned with what is mine. "This is my house. It has 3,400 square feet and we need every inch. You remember when we made that trip to Europe. I saw so many great antiques I just had to have them all. And, the four car garage . . . well I have the SUV and the minivan but, you know . . . I also found that little red sports car I always wanted, so . . . well there it is. We had to have the space. And . . . the speed-boat has to go in there too. 'Course, I can't leave the boat docked at the lake cottage all winter. I'm going to add a boat house next spring." And on and on with me—mine—and—I. The words I might use to acknowledge him are:

- Father, you are my king in every part of my life; you are everywhere and I welcome you everywhere that I am or may be.
- Father, your kingdom is everywhere. Permit me to be with you in your kingdom.
- Father, I acknowledge you're everywhere and everywhere is yours.
- Father, I am walking toward your home, your kingdom, where you are king. May your kingdom exist forever.

We are called to recognize God's sovereignty and his kingdom is all there is and it is everywhere. It is like saying, "Air is everywhere and everywhere there is air there is life. Wherever there is not air, there is no life."

Do not misunderstand. I am not saying God is air. He created air and all there is. I use air only as an illustration.

Now, honor God and his omnipresence, his "every-where-ness," in your own words. Or, express it as, "It is God's kingdom to which we are on our journey of life," if that meets your understanding of theology.

- 

- 

-

### He is Here All the Time

"After a little while the world will no longer see Me, but you will see Me; because I live, you will live also. In that day you will know that I am in My Father, and you in Me, and I in you." John 14: 19-20 NIV

"Why does God seem so distant sometimes?" Have you heard someone ask that question? I have.

Jesus said, even when the world cannot see him anymore, he will be in God, and we will be in him and he will be in us. Reread that. Not just that we will be in him, although that is a marvelous thing, but he will be in us and in God. Therefore, we will also be in God and he in us.

If anyone has moved in this great triangular fellowship, we have. God remains the same. He is not distant from us. We choose to be distant from him. Just remember, he is here all the time. Let us pray:

"Father, God, you are the rock that anchors me to heaven, to the Christ and to you. You never move away, nor do you sleep. I've been aware that some are ill or sick of heart. You are peace, Father, and Jesus is with you and I am with you both. Lay your hand of comfort on me, my friends and family, so that we may feel your healing. I know that you have far greater plans for me than any I could imagine. My length of days is written in your book. I also believe though my days are numbered here, eternity lies within you, and that is where I am, too. Forgive my need to wish for lesser things than the golden streets of Heaven. I want what you want, Father. I give up my need to try to control you and ask that you be my guide and shepherd. In the name of, and by the power of, Jesus, your son, I pray. Amen"
Doris

Posted and Copyrighted Doris Gaines Rapp at www.prayertherapyrapp.blogspot.com on 9-15-14

## Chapter 11

**Honor God's Omnipotence: . . . *and the power . . .***

Here, the Lord's Prayer directs our attention to the power of God and what follows: that his power may last forever. We recognize God has always been and he will always be. That does not mean we have the ability to understand his omnipotence. Can we possibly fathom that anything or anyone, even God, has always been and ever will be? That he is outside of time. He is not bound by time, measured by time, nor does he relate to us within the framework of earth's time.

Look how long it took, in earth-time, to bring the promised Messiah to earth.

Think of how long the children of Israel wandered in the desert—forty years! It would seem they would have looked up, at some point, and would have seen the same stars in the same area of the night sky and realized something was wrong, long before forty years had passed. Nevertheless, God's plan was being accomplished and time was not relevant to his efforts. He could have had the Israelites wander for four-hundred and forty years, and it still would have accomplished his purpose for his children.

We think God's promise means he will provide our wants and desires in an instant, when we snap our fingers and want immediate gratification. When we are in God's kingdom, within his walls, we are on his time-table, or better put, outside of time as we know it.

You are probably saying, "How do you expect me to understand that?"

My response is, "I don't expect you to understand it at all. I know I certainly don't. It is enough for me to know that God understands. It is God who has all the power, not either of us.

Young people, teens, struggle for their power, for their own voice. They want to take control of their lives, yet their parents tell them, "We still know better." It is very difficult for them to depend on their parents for everything, when they are at an age where independence is their goal. Harmony can come to their home when they yield their power to their parents for a little longer, while they gain the education that will give them the earning power to secure their own independence. Living in harmony also means that parents respect the young adults living in their home.

While it is the parents' home, it is understood, except for the need for education, these young adults would have been out of the parental home and on their own.

While still at home, the young people yield to the "house rules" because the parents still hold the power. We yield our struggle for power to God because God holds the ultimate power. It is at this point in our prayer that we acknowledge God's complete power, and pray his power will be present forever.

Regarding very small children, many parents went through an era in child rearing when experts admonished us for telling our children "Do it because I said so." They cautioned, "The little darlings need and deserve a respectful explanation of our demands on them." We found ourselves explaining to toddlers why they should not touch fire. We were talking too much when a simple, "No," was sufficient and even more effective.

It is often enough that we parents know "why," without complex reasoning. Children soon learn selective listening, when we talk on and on. Since they don't understand what we're talking about, why listen to words, words, words. The same is true with God. It is enough he knows all, and has the power to implement his plan. We yield ourselves to his power even when we do not know what yielding may mean.

Thinking about ways to write statements of acknowledgment of his power, I have tried to express my amazement of God's power in these words:

- You, Father, are all powerful and I pray your power endures forever.
- I am weak, Father, and you are strong and powerful.
- Your power is above anything I could possibly imagine.
- You hold the power of this universe and every universe in your own hands. May it always be so.
- Father, I seek no power for myself, only that you have total power in my life.
- All praise to you, Father God, who holds the power of our time and every time in your mighty hands.

It is a simple task, but who we are praising is far from simple. We are relinquishing any desire for power of our own and claiming that God's power is sufficient for us. And, we honor it by our prayer that it may endure forever. Now take some time to write a few statements of your own.

-

-

-

-

-

## SOULS SPRING FORTH LIKE FRAGRANT BLOSSOMS

"Then Jehoshaphat stood in the assembly of Judah and Jerusalem, in the house of the LORD before the new court, and said: "LORD, the God of our ancestors, are you not the God who is in heaven? You rule over all the kingdoms of the nations. Power and might are in your hand, and no one can withstand you. " 2 Chronicles 20:5-6 NIV

Have you seen the change in color all around us? The brilliance of God's good earth is everywhere! His blessing of beauty is like a reward for the plain and dull winter we go through. Do you remember the first snow of the last season? Wasn't it wonderful and clean and bright? But, soon the white turned to dirty gray and the slush piled up like rubble heaps in the corners of shopping malls, marring the reflecting pools nearby.

That is so much like many of our lives. The precious infant, who began life with the promise of all that would be good and beautiful as an adult, sometimes turns dark and gets pushed to the margins of life, unloved and unwanted. While that is all true, the miracle of rebirth in the spring is a yearly reminder that life can be brought back to a hopeful beginning again.

No matter how dark the stain, how cold the heart, or how sluggish the mind, the soul can spring forth again in a new beginning, with a new meaning, and a fresh purpose—to love Him and to spread that love to all those around us. Let us pray:

"Holy Father, God of all there is, I stand in awe at the beauty you share with me in the springtime of my life. Thank you that spring can come at any age, under any circumstances, and regardless of any secret ice that has chilled my heart. Your holiness can melt any cold shoulder and clean any blot on the beautiful garments of life you have given me. Like ladies of old,

who held their head high as their skirt-tail drug through the filthy streets, the garments you give me come clean each new day, when my head and heart remain above the slush and swill of the world. Dirty shoes only mean I have labored in your streets. A filthy heart means that the streets have found their way inside my soul, like a cold wind that snaps through the cracks around me. You, oh God, have blessed me with the beauty of spring, a visible witness to your grace and forgiveness. Forgive me when I only see the dirty, dark caves of life and not the diamonds that glitter on the walls. With gold comes back-breaking mining; with fragrant flowers comes the rain. Thank you Father, for all your precious blossoms that bloom all around me, which I forget to take the time to see, and am not humble enough to bend low to touch the petals. Thank you for the spring of my life that comes after every bitter season. May I always look for the sweetness of each new day, which follows the time of night. I pray in the name of your precious son, Jesus, who sprang up again like the lilies of the field from a night of death and a time of sorrow. To you, oh God, be all glory and honor and praise. Amen"
Doris
Posted and Copyrighted Doris Gaines Rapp at www.prayertherapyrapp.blogspot.com on 4-19-10

Chapter 12

**Relinquishing Credit Back To God:** *. . . and the glory forever.*

Do we really have to add this part to our prayer? Yes, we do! Jesus knew exactly how we would be, how we always are. We want the glory . . . even when we are participating in God's work!

One Monday morning, I sat around a table with a group of ministers, listening to a conversation that sounded like this:

Pastor One: "Wow, I'm beat today. We had such a big service yesterday."

Pastor Two: "I know what you mean. We had three-hundred twenty-five people in worship."

Pastor Three: "I heard you're growing. We had to go to two services, over two-hundred in each."

Pastor Four: "I remember those days, trying to build up that second service can be hard, but I know you can do it. We were pushing out the walls and went to two services, now we pack them in at both."

Pastor One: "I hear you. We had over seven-hundred in all services yesterday."

Need I go on further? As you can see, numbers were all that was important to these ministers of the gospel-of-self-glory. However, numbers mean nothing except as a measure of self-glorification. If there had been one soul who had found their way back to God on Sunday morning, and no-one else showed up, all the saints in heaven would have rejoiced. Each soul is unique and precious—not just one of a group or congregation. We are only, and I repeat, ONLY servants of the Master who heals, forgives, and saves. And, to God's glory, we have the deep privilege of being servants of the Master who restores, reprieves, and reconciles. When we lead someone to the Lord, we do nothing except point in the direction of Calvary. Numbers are completely irrelevant at the foot of the cross. One is enough and any number above one is also enough, enough until *God* claims another, not us. We cite numbers only to bring glory to ourselves.

Souls are won, one at a time—by God, and to the glory of God, not our own acclaim.

This is a very important point because when we do not give credit where credit is due, we not only dishonor God; we turn away those who would have been turned toward Christ. The world recognizes a power-hungry, glory-seeking follower of self-interests, even if we do not have eyes to discern it in ourselves.

Give God the glory, just as Jesus instructed us to do, and may his glory endure forever and ever. Then, God can work through us, because we will have gotten out of his way.

Now it is time for you and me to give all glory back to where it always was, in God's powerful hands. Think for a few minutes. I will go first and then you follow.

- Father, I relinquish back any claim to glory I secretly hold on to.
- May all glory be given to you Father, both now and forever.
- Please Father, may I be invisible and may your love shine through.
- All glory is yours Father, forever. May I realize that down at the very core of my being.
- I want no glory for myself, Father. I want only that your face be recognized through me.
- I do not wear glory well, Father. Only you are wise enough to take it on. I give it all to you and may it always be so.

Alright, I know it may be harder for some of us than others. But, claiming glory is futile anyway. It has never been ours and it never will be. When we claim it for our own, we are only hijacking God's glory from him and tarnishing it beyond recognition with our greedy hands. It can only be beautiful and glorious when it resides with God. Take some time and express relinquishing any claim to glory back to God.

- 
- 
- 
- 
- 
-

## THE GOD BRAND

"Worship the LORD with gladness; come before him with joyful songs. Know that the LORD is God. It is he who made us, and we are his; we are his people, the sheep of his pasture. Enter his gates with thanksgiving and his courts with praise; give thanks to him and praise his name. For the LORD is good and his love endures forever; his faithfulness continues through all generations." Psalm 100: 2-5

Why do some Christians take on an "ownership" attitude where God is concerned? They believe they have all the correct answers. They even claim to have the only questions as well. All other beliefs in God are therefore incorrect, right down to half dozen or so words that are acceptable. If those buzz words aren't used, and used correctly in their mind, you cannot possibly be a Christian. They have taken on the God/Christ Brand.

"If I look just right, and talk correctly, I can be successful in the Christian community." That is not Christianity my friend. That is commercializing the name of the Holy One, trying to acquire His brand.

If our relationship with God doesn't start with humbling ourselves to His will and following His lead, then we will have to find another name for it. I don't know what to call it, and even if I could guess, I would be defaming the body of Christ, the same as the people I first mentioned. The only window we can peer into, to evaluate a person's faith, is the mirror. The only ministry we have is that of witness, bearing testimony to the work of God in our own lives.

If we must have a "brand" to define our lives, let it be "servant," not "He/she who knows the mind of God." Faith in God is a relationship, a sacred connection. It is not joining a social network to advance our climb to the top. Let us pray for a humble heart and a bold approach to fulfilling the work He has given us.

"Holy Father, shine your light from heaven and set your flame in my heart. Your name is holy to my ears. May your kingdom come in your time. I humbly ask to be your servant. I would rather sweep up the crumbs from under your table than to be left out of your banquet hall. To live within your love, in any capacity, is better than living a moment in darkness. Forgive me when I have tried to use your name for my own benefit. Your name is to be called on to help and heal others. Like others, I know someone who is alone and hurting; I call on your love to come and brush away their tears and heal their broken heart. May I be humbly bold, to testify to your love. I pray that all glory be yours, oh Father. In the name of Jesus Christ I pray. Amen"
Doris
"God gives us stories that testify to His love. Let me tell you mine."
Posted and Copyrighted Doris Gaines Rapp at www.prayertherapyrapp.blogspot.com on 6-27-11

Chapter 13

**Closing: "*Amen*"**

Webster's New Collegiate Dictionary defines "Amen" in these words, "amen—used to express solemn ratification (as of an expression of faith) or hearty approval (as of an assertion)."

When we close our prayers with the word "Amen," we are expressing our belief in what we have prayed. We affirm our faith in the reality that God hears our pray and will honor our petition. I did not say he would grant all of our wishes. He is not our personal genie in a jug, granting all our wishes. He is the Almighty.

"Amen," is not simply, "Good-bye God," or "Over and out" or "Ten - four."

"Amen" means we have prayed earnestly, honestly and are in agreement with the words of what we have prayed. And, we have faith in the God to whom we have prayed.

While "Amen" is all we need to say, if we are giving our hearty approval to our prayer, we will take the time to put our closing in our own words. In this way, we insure that we truly understand the concept. The following are the words I have chosen:

- May it be so.
- So shall it be.
- Please, let it be so.
- I close, asking honestly that my prayer be heard and by faith I know it has been heard.

- Thank you God, for hearing and honoring my earnest prayer.

It may seem silly to find other words, or more words, to express what is usually spoken in one word, "Amen." But, I know I found it quite insightful looking for an expansion of the short-hand. Give it a try and I pray you are blessed as well with a deeper understanding of what we have previously prayed automatically.

Chapter 14

**Claiming Christ's Power:** *In the name of Jesus Christ. Or, by the power* **of** *Jesus Christ.*

As we just observed, we have no power. We have yielded our power over to God's will that His power might shine through. We claim God's power in our lives and in the lives of our loved ones, through the name of Jesus Christ. We are inheritors of all God has, as his children, through the blood of Jesus Christ. We cannot demand that God yield his power to us in return. We claim his power through the line of our Master, our Savior, the one we follow, Jesus Christ.

It would be similar to our going to our neighbor's house and collecting the subscription money for the local newspaper. We are not there to ask for money for our own use. We are there, in the name of the local paper.

"Good Evening Mrs. Jones. I'm collecting for the EVENING NEWS (in the name of and by the authority of that newspaper). That will be five ninety-five. Thank you and have a good evening."

We have no power of our own to solicit money from our neighbors. We are there using another's authority and power, in this case, the local newspaper.

When we pray to God, we are not making our petitions because we are worthy, or because we have any power to influence God. We pray using the authority and power of God's son, Jesus Christ. We have already recognized we have no power and God's power is the only true power in all of creation. We certainly could not go to God in prayer based on any merit of our own. We dare to go to God in prayer because Jesus told us to use his name. His worthiness qualifies us as Jesus's followers.

It is a simple statement at the end of our prayers but it has enormous meaning. Since we have no power and Jesus's power is sufficient for us, we cannot possibly claim credit for answered prayer. It is Jesus who is praised, not us.

It is also at this point in our prayer where we have the opportunity to wait for God to reveal himself to us. Praying in the name of and by the power of Jesus Christ gives us the opportunity to rest in the assurance that God hears our prayers since he is the father of our Lord and therefore our father. We can seize the moment to wait upon him to reveal himself to us so we may know we are in his presence. We are then to go out, living expectantly, knowing God has heard our prayers. He will answer our prayers in his own time and in his own way.

As I think about the Almighty hearing my prayers and petitions, it never ceases to fill me with awe. He listens to even me, because I do not stand before him alone. I stand in the protective relationship of his son Jesus. I have chosen the following words to ask for Jesus to intercede for me:

- I humbly pray to you in the name of and by the power of your son, Jesus Christ.
- Although I am unworthy to ask for anything in my own name, I ask that you bless my request through the name of Jesus Christ, your son, my savior.
- My motives are imperfect Father. Please listen to my prayers in the perfect name of Jesus. I accept that my words may have to be remolded to be in line with your will.
- Not my will but your will be done in my life, through the power of Jesus.
- I want to want nothing in my life but what you want, Father. May I really desire that with no reservations.

Now, put your thoughts into words that would express your desire to have Jesus intercede in your life and in your actions, wants, and plans.

- 

- 

- 

- 

- 

Now we will call by name, those negative emotions that bind us and keep us captive. Like calling out a bully, to deflate their power and rid them of their control over our lives, we name each painful emotion and pray for release from them, so God can hear our specific request and respond to our daily needs.

Chapter 15

**Negative Emotions**

**ANGER**

Anger is the first negative emotion I will describe. We have all experienced some form of anger. Sometimes it's hard for us to admit we're angry. We may say, "I am not angry. I'm just frustrated." Other times we may not be able to admit the anger to ourselves or to others, but our body language betrays our real feelings.

Do you remember a parent or teacher shouting at you, "I am not angry," all the while their face is taut and tense, their hands are squarely and firmly anchored to their hips, and their entire body inclines toward you like a bull moose ready to charge? "No," they protest, "I am not angry." You know they're angry because you can read their body-language—which speaks louder than their words.

The rule of thumb is if we receive two messages from someone, one verbal and one non-verbal, it's the non-verbal message that gives away the true, inner emotions . . . the true message.

I remember my sixth grade teacher lecturing me on my incomplete work assignments. I had been given the privilege of working in the principal's office for about hour that day. And, our principal, Miss Rose Miller was an institution within the larger institution of education at Pasadena Grade School. Her hair was pulled back in a grey/white bun and her loosely fitting gray flowered dresses hung nearly to the top of her black leather laced-up oxford shoes. She had quite an under-bite and wore no make-up. She could have been easily mistaken for a feisty bull dog or Broom-Hilda ready for flight . . . but I loved her. She was as gruff as a grizzly bear and as gentle as a devoted grandmother, all at the same time. And, she was always fair. When she called out your name in the hall or cafeteria, you did not wonder who she was talking to. Her volume and intonation made it perfectly clear. There was nothing vague about Rose Miller.

I was so proud I had the opportunity to work in the office, filing papers for her. However, I hadn't completed my seat work in my classroom before I went to the principal's office . . . a major mistake. When I returned to my classroom, my sixth grade teacher, Mrs. Haas, demanded in a stern voice, "Who do you think you are?" She didn't demand such an existential question of an eleven-year-old because she was mean, but because she expected better of me.

That seems like a hundred and fifty years ago, but my memory is quite good.

I'll always remember that I didn't know how to respond. I didn't even know if I was expected to say anything at all. Since that day, I have made it my goal to have an answer to that question should anyone ask again. I have often reminded myself, "Who do I think I am? I know myself to be a child of the living Father, the father of my Lord and Savior Jesus Christ. I am a wife, a mother, a sister, a daughter and a friend. I am a psychologist and author. I am the person God intended me to be, although rough at times and unpolished." Mrs. Haas challenged me to know who I am. Perhaps that was not her intent, but it was the result of her question. For that, I will always thank her.

Anger, and one's response to anger, can be a catalyst to change, a change in oneself. Anger can be the flame that ignites a fire to correct a wrong, a wrong done against oneself, another, or society as a whole. But, anger can also leave one defensive and/or in a fighting mode—when a battle is inappropriate. If someone makes us angry, or we are in a situation that could provoke anger, we mirror the same posture just described and take on the bodily stance of "anger."

That posture is tense and tight and will leave you exhausted if you remain in that pose for very long. One of the ways hidden anger may be identified is to determine the answer to the question, "Am I tired from the battle at the end of the day?"

Headaches, stomach upsets, tense muscles, can all be bodily clues that one is nurturing anger. Family members may tell you, "You seem to be angry all of the time."

In Prayer Therapy we pray as Jesus taught us to pray, prescriptively, three times a day. Just as medication from our physician heals our bodies, our prescription of prayer heals our anger. In the portion of the prayer where we are instructed to pray for our "daily bread," or that which we need for that day, we include our specific request for release from anger. Over many months of praying, we will begin to see a change in our lives as we become freed from the prison of anger.

During prayer time, following words of adoration and petition wait quietly for an awareness of God's presence. During that quiet time, close your eyes and see the peace that freedom from anger brings. Picture it in many ways. You may wish to think of a blue-white light, the love of God, filling and overflowing you until the light shoots out of your hair and finger tips. That is the Light of God as might be imagined. We might feel the softness of fur or silk and think of God's tenderness and love. That tenderness drives out anger and replaces it with the Love that has filled us. Choose one of these visual representations of the peace of God, or think of one with which you can better identify. Hold that image in your mind after you pray for the release of anger from your life.

What might a prayer for the release of anger look like? Read the one I have written; then, practice one on your own. Remember to follow the style of the Lord's Prayer in all its detail. Also, "waiting quietly on the Lord," for the assurance of his presence and knowing he has heard us, is an important part of prayer. It is God's energy that assures us we can go forth throughout the day, knowing he has heard our prayer.

**Prayer for Release from ANGER**

"Oh Father, God of all, your precious name I praise. May your kingdom come swiftly to restore us to you and may your will be done in my life as it is with the Angels in heaven. I humbly ask you, Father that you rid my life of anger and deliver me from anger's grip. Cast my anger into the deepest pit and never let it return to me. Forgive me for angry outbursts I have leveled against others and, shamefully, against you. May I be as generous in my forgiving of others' anger as you are with me. Protect me with your mighty hands, so that anger may never have a chance to get near me again. You are the master of all there is. You hold the power of the universe in your strong hands. And, I pray, Father, it may always be so. In the precious name of your son, my savior, Jesus, I pray. Amen."

**Jealousy**

Jealousy is a problem many experience. When our daughter, Kathleen was two or three years old, she would admit she was feeling "jelly." By that, she meant she was jealous of a situation regarding her younger sister, Amanda.

Even though you and I aren't toddlers, when we feel jealous, we can also feel a little "jelly," reduced to a formless mass of hurt feelings with no real definition, just a desire for something we do not have, that we see another does possess. We spill over our own boundaries and merge with another, never satisfied with what we have but long for what another has. Unlike fruit jelly or preserves, however, we are anything but sweet. We may even harbor resentment because another has that coveted "thing" which we do not have. We may believe the other person does not deserve to have the "thing" if we can't have it too. Often, we wish we could have the "thing," while the other person does not.

The fact that we are describing, "things," rather than our blessings, might give an immediate clue that our priorities are in the wrong place. An accumulation of "things" has never brought true happiness.

*Prayer Therapy of Jesus*                                        Doris Gaines Rapp, Ph.D.

We go to God in Prayer Therapy, asking for release from jealously, three times per day. Within the Lord's Prayer template, when we come to the portion:

"Give us this day our daily bread," we substitute our request for bread, for our specific prayer for release from jealousy.

**Prayer for Release from JEALOUSY**

"Our Father in the high heavens, I worship you on bended knee. May your kingdom begin in my heart until your son, Jesus, comes again to usher into Heaven. I admit I am jealous of others and I ask you, Father, to release me from the jealously that grips my heart and robs me of the joy others experience, as well as my own peace and contentment. Turn my head away from a focus on what others have, so I may see and rejoice in all the blessings you have given me. All that is, belongs to you, Father. I only borrow what I need while I am here. Your generous hand has given me everything and for that I give you all praise and glory. I pray in the name of your son, Jesus, who gave up the peace of Heaven to come to save even me. Amen."

Then, while we wait quietly for his presence to be revealed to us, we could close our eyes and see Jesus Christ beside us as we stand with the one of whom we are jealous. See Jesus taking your hand and placing it in the hand of the other person, then he covers both of your hands with his own. Feel his healing and his unity. Then, go about the remainder of the day living as though you know your prayer has been heard.

**Fear**

Fear is the third negative emotion that robs us of our ability to serve God.

There are two kinds of fear, justified fear and unjustified fear. We may be afraid of walking alone after dark through a dark alley. Great! We should be afraid of dangerous situations. However, some of us have unfounded fear.

We could search and search and would not be able to find a real reason for our fear.

Some are afraid of being in front of a group, of speaking up or speaking out.

There is no real reason for their fear. No one is going to harm them if they speak. Quite to the contrary. Most people are quick to encourage another to participate, to speak out, and to join in. People who do not want another to succeed are suffering from their own fears—perhaps a fear that says, "If s/he joins in, I will be left out."

Some people are afraid to succeed because they fear their friends or parents may expect more from them in the future—more than they could give. So, rather than the possibility of having to give more and more, they choose to not try at all. That is a fear of success.

Others are afraid, if they try, they will lose anyway. So, rather than trying and losing, they don't try in the first place. These people have a fear of failure.

Some lonely souls are afraid to love because they have been hurt in the past. Therefore, they choose to keep people at a distance. This could also be generalized to the fear of losing, or a fear of abandonment.

There are some young adults who are afraid to leave home, so they set themselves up to fail at college. They would rather be a college drop-out than feel the fear they experience from being away from home.

While I directed a University Counseling Center, I counseled with a very gifted young freshman co-ed who was so home-sick she was contemplating leaving college. Her parents had told her she couldn't take her car to college the first year. They also said she had to stay on campus until Thanksgiving rather than going home, so she could get acclimated to college life and make friends. With her permission, I called her parents and worked out an alternative plan for her. Her parents agreed she could come home every weekend and she would be permitted to have her car on campus, giving her the transportation to drive home.

The result was as I expected. By giving her the option of coming home every weekend and providing the transportation to do so, she no longer had the need to go home. She had options. She could go home if she wanted to, her car was waiting for her in the parking lot, or she could stay on campus. By giving her options, she was free to make her own decision. During the following month, she went home about every other weekend. Her trips home tapered off in subsequent months with more involvement with new residence hall friends and campus activities. It was not that she was homesick. The issue was her fear of feeling trapped, of having no options. Due to that fear, she was driven to run.

There is also a new phenomenon among young people, a fear of making a commitment in relationships. In counseling with young Christians, I continue to find they're so afraid of divorce they are incapable of committing to marriage.

Too frequently, Christian young adults are engaging in pre-marital sex as a substitute for marriage. Their bodies and drives were created to unite with a partner and make a life-time commitment to marriage. However, their fear of failure keeps them from committing themselves to another.

The dilemma is: (1) Their Christian mentors are telling them to wait until age thirty to marry, while the mentors go home to loving spouses and warm beds. (2) The world tells them to observe animals that don't mate for life, so why should they expect to do so. Society cautions—chances for marital success are limited. Fear grips their heart rather than love.

We would all agree that a college education is necessary to secure a strong financial foundation. However, life-building after college is better done together in a Christian marriage. Working together in a committed relationship will help solidify the concept of "ours," rather than "yours-and-mine." Making a commitment to each other—to pray, work, grow, and play together as husband and wife—helps dissipate fear and fosters maturity. Holding on to childhood fantasies—(1) having life the way we want it (immaturity), such as intimacy without marriage, and (2) life needs to center around us and our own needs (self-centeredness)—are neither Biblical nor exemplary of a Spirit-filled life.

As to our "animal instincts," a moment's reflection will remind us that humans are above the animals. As believers in God, we were called to dominate over our animal tendencies. If those in the world wish to see themselves as no more than evolved animals, we as Christian should know better. We are filled with the Holy Spirit and the Spirit of God has power over the world.

Fear takes many forms. Look into your own heart and life, and see where fear handcuffs you with chains of suspicion, mistrust and dismay, and binds you with shackles of cowardliness, hesitation, and non-commitment.

How can we overcome our fear? In Prayer Therapy, we pray three times a day for release from the fear that binds us. We don't have to be specific about the result of fear, such as, "Help me, Father, make commitments and keep them."

Instead, we pray for release from specific negative emotions, the basic underlying emotional manacle of FEAR. During the portion of prayer where we pray for "daily bread" (daily needs), we pray for release from FEAR.

**Prayer for Release from FEAR**

"Oh Father, strong and powerful, you hold lightening in your grasp. Your name calms my fears and stills my frightened heart. May your majesty fill all the earth as heaven is now blessed, both at the time of your son's return and even now in my heart. Like a frightened child, I pray you will rid me of the fear that holds my spirit, as would a loving father. Forgive me when my knees have been weak and have buckled under fear, when I have not trusted you to deliver me. May I never bring fear to others but help those who also fear this world. Lead me away from fearful pitfalls and deliver me safely on the other side. You are the author of strength. You hold power in your mighty hands, both now and forever. I give all glory to you, Father, and your precious Son, Jesus my savior, in and through whom I pray. Amen."

For imagery, you might remember Daniel, our hero from the Old Testament, as he stared down the lion in the king's den of torture. Or, you might see the humble, loving Jesus, looking death in the face as he stood before Pilate. Jesus denied nothing when he was brought before Pilate. He stood unafraid, wrapped in the secure love of his Father, God.

Choose a memory of someone who has faced fear and overcame its hold on them. You might also choose a memory in your past in which you were successful in conquering fear and see God integrate that success into your present life, like merging two documents on a computer into one. Then, thank God for answering your prayer for release from FEAR and wait patiently to feel his peace. Now, go out rejoicing in God's steadfastness in hearing your prayer.

**Self-Hate**

Self-hate also cripples our ability to speak out for God. These concepts may seem a little far afield to you. Still, it is necessary that we look at the issue of self-hate. Those who hate themselves find it impossible to fully love others.

Some people may call it low self-esteem. I have chosen to label it self-hate.

When one does not value the earthly body or personality God has given them, or the person they have become or are becoming, they are engaging in a level of self-hate. Perhaps you prefer self-dislike, maybe even low self-esteem.

Many are not satisfied with their body unless it is perfect. Some are convinced others are more creative, more loving, kinder, smarter, and on and on.

Our body is our dwelling place, given to us on loan from God. Our body gives our Spirit form and shape, hands to do God's work, mouths to give testimony to God's work within us, and feet to carry our testimony to others. Our body keeps our Spirit anchored to the earth, our home away from home. Without it, we would float back to Heaven to be with God.

What do some do? They complain to God he didn't give them a taller or shorter body, a thinner or heavier body, formed, sculpted, and shaped just as the world defines beauty. God has made a mistake, many moan! They claim to be wiser than God and they will correct his mistakes through plastic surgery, abuse, or starvation of the loathed body.

As to other attributes—a capacity to love, an innate intelligence, creativity—these are all gifts God has given us in order to be of service to him. Some too often use these gifts for self-service, to draw attention to them in an effort to make them feel more important than others. Deep within, they really feel less important than others, because they simply do not like themselves. What a circle of confusion.

A young woman once told me, "But I have no talents. I can't sing. I can't speak in public. I can't draw or paint. I can't do anything."

Yet that same young woman has the warmest smile and brightest attitude of anyone I know, when she isn't defeating herself with self-hate. Too often, the parents of a self-hater are blamed for their child's dislike turned inward. We know many of these children are born with an inherited tendency to blame themselves, to esteem themselves not, and to find fault with their own gifts and hold them in lower value than another's gifts. We are born with the personality we have as adults. Our personality is similar to our parents, even if we are adopted and have never lived with our birth parents.

Sometimes, the Church teaches that we are not to develop our self-esteem because the members claim it means we place ourselves above others and esteem ourselves to be of greater value than they.

We aren't to value ourselves above another. We value ourselves as equal to all others. Someone with a positive self-esteem can value themselves, as God values them and therefore treat others as equals.

Jean Ellsley Clarke, a writer in the area of self-esteem, said, "Blessed are the self-esteemers for they have seen the beauty of their own souls." Self-esteemers can see the Creator behind the created and love God's creation. That is not to raise oneself above others. It is to value oneself to the same degree we value others.

"Love your neighbor as yourself," can be transformed to, "Love yourself as you love your neighbor." That is positive self-esteem. Many people, however, find it very difficult to like, much less love themselves.

Using the Prayer Therapy method to rid ourselves of Self-Hate, go to God in prayer three times a day, as is now our pattern, praying for release from the specific, underlying problem.

**Prayer for Release from SELF-HATE**

"Father God, ruler of my soul, I bow before your pure love and worship you, as impure as I am. May your kingdom come swiftly and usher in the glorious day of your reign, as Heaven now enjoys your perfect plan. I ask you, Father God, to release me from the self-hate that binds me and prevents me from seeing the beautiful soul within me that only you could have created. Forgive me for not holding dear the life you have given me and all other aspects of myself you created. May I always see your beauty in all of those around me, for I know, where there are those who love you, there is beauty. I pray I may not yield to the temptation of slipping again into old patterns of self-hate and deliver me from the evil-one's lies about me. For you are the ruler of my eyes and heart and can cause beauty to be seen in me. You are almighty and have the power to release me from self-hate's grip. To you I give the praise, for only you deserve the glory. In the precious name of your beautiful son, my savior, Jesus, I pray. Amen."

Then, you might close your eyes and see yourself as an ugly troll, bound in chains under a cobblestone bridge, visited there, in your misery and self-loathing, by the radiant God our Father. As he touches you and springs the lock that seals your chains, see yourselves transformed into the beautiful soul God created in the first place. He frees you from your self-hating perception of yourselves and gives you the ability to see yourself as he sees you, his beautiful creation. Wait there while the radiance of his presence fills you to overflowing. Then, rise and live the day knowing he has heard your prayers and you are beautiful in his sight.

**Anxiety**

Anxiety keeps us from offering the name of Jesus to another. Anxiety is a very uncomfortable, all-encompassing feeling, that one doesn't have control over their body. They may be shaky, jittery inside, and have other motor tension. They may experience a sense of impending doom.

They could experience sweating; heart pounding or racing; cold, clammy hands; dry mouth; and dizziness. They may feel apprehension such as worry, rumination, and anticipation of misfortunes to come. They may be hyper-vigilant or have difficulty concentrating, experience insomnia, irritability and/or impatience.

Anxiety takes two forms: specific anxiety and generalized anxiety. The anxiety just described is Generalized Anxiety. One is anxious but does not know why they feel as they do.

Examples of specific anxiety or phobia are a fear of flying in airplanes or a fear of animals, such as dogs. You may be afraid of leaving your home, as in Agoraphobia. Or, you may have a Social Phobia such as a fear you will embarrass yourself by doing something ridiculous in public, even though you know it is unrealistic to hold that fear.

You may suffer from Panic Attacks, or identifiable periods of panic with rapid heart rate, heaviness in your chest, dizziness or vertigo, sweaty palms, trembling/shaking, or faintness.

These episodes do not last indefinitely but seem to come over you, last for a time, and then pass. However, while you are in a Panic Attack you may feel as though you may die from the symptoms.

Obsessions or obsessive thoughts are also a form of anxiety. When you obsess, you cannot rid yourself of unwanted thoughts. As uncomfortable as the thoughts are, you rehearse them over and over in your head. The more you rehearse the thoughts, the more obsessed you become. And, the more obsessive you are, the more you rehearse those very obsessive thoughts.

Using Prayer Therapy, pray for release from the ANXIETY that binds you. Set your mind and body free and find calmness in the Lord.

**Prayer for Release from ANXIETY**

"Lord God, father of my savior, Jesus, your name is above all names for you are precious to me. I pray your kingdom may come in my lifetime so you can reign supreme, while all other earthly things which draw my attention and adoration fade away. Only then, can I live in peace as do the angels in heaven. I pray you will release me from the grip of anxiety in all its forms. Drive out thoughts I cannot control. Cast out the panic that takes over my body and leaves me panting and afraid, so I will not die in my misery. Unleash me from the anxiety that has me tied in knots as I try to depend on you. My heart is willing, but I cannot seem to will my body to follow my heart; for, I do not hold power over the evil-one on my own. Only you, God, have power over evil. Forgive me when I cause others to be anxious with my unreasonable demands or impatience and block my reaction to those who treat me the same way. Lead me through the chasm of anxiety, calm my heart with your peace and deliver me, peacefully and contented on the other side of anxiety. For all these blessings, I will give you all the glory, both now and forever more. In the name of, and by the power of your only son, Jesus Christ, I pray. Amen."

Then, you might close your eyes and see yourself as a quivering mass of humanity, shaking from anxiety in comic-book exaggeration, shaking and wobbling like a tuning fork that has just been struck. Then, see Jesus wrap his arms all the way around you, calming your tremors and stilling your anxious heart. The request is simple. The result of this prayer is freedom, freedom from chains that bind you in anxiety.

In many cases, people are so under the grip of anxiety they require an antianxiety medication, as prescribed by their physician. Do not avoid a consideration of medication for anxiety because you feel it may indicate a lack of belief in prayer, and God's ability to heal. God gave these medications to mankind through the research of physicians and scientists. We must take the next step of healing by implementing a program of prayer for the medication's effectiveness and the success of our body in responding to the medication.

Perhaps we may be able to shorten the time we need to remain on the medication through our belief in God who hears and heals.

**Depression**

When we are depressed, we have no energy to follow the Lord's call. Depression robs us of our sleep and happiness. When we are depressed, we often wake up about two or three a.m. and find we cannot go back to sleep.

Or, we may sleep all night but wake up as tired, or even more tired, as when we went to bed. We usually feels lethargic (draggy and without energy) and unable to concentrate on our work. We may feel inadequate and unable to accomplish anything of value. We may lose interest in activities we had previously enjoyed such as sports, exercise, crafts, conversations and activities with friends, or reading. We may lose interest in sexual relations with our spouse and feel we lack the energy to even care anymore. We may be withdrawn or unwilling or unable to be around other people. We may be pessimistic or negative about the future. Often, we have no plans for the future, lacking a future orientation or interest beyond "now." Also, those of us who are depressed may be very tearful and unable to control our "sad" emotions.

A symptom not as easily recognized but is often seen in children and adolescents who are depressed, is anger, with angry outbursts and "acting out."

Examples of "acting out" would be "doing" inappropriate activities such as running away from home or becoming sexually promiscuous.

Some who are depressed have suicide ideation or thoughts, and may even attempt suicide. A few succeed in suicide during their lowest period. Suicide potential must be assessed by a professional psychologist or psychiatrist, to protect the individual from harming themselves.

Depression must be taken seriously. Telling a depressed person, "Just pull yourself together," is neither helpful nor possible. As I tell clients who claim they "should" be able to heal themselves, "If you could have, you would have. But, you couldn't so you didn't."

A depressed family member needs professional help—counseling as well as a consultation with a physician for an evaluation for medication. Some may require hospitalization until severe depression is treated and the patient is stabilized on medication.

If you or a family member suffers from any of the above symptoms of depression, seek professional help. If your child's grades drop, or they drop out of previously enjoyed activities, take notice. Talk to them about it.

You don't have to experience a difficult time of life—like the great disappointment of losing a scholarship or breaking up with a boy/girlfriend—to become depressed. A chemically based depression can creep in when life is otherwise going well. A chemically based depression is a depressive state caused by an imbalance in a specific neurotransmitter substance in the brain. This endogenous condition is often inherited or genetic. It often does not need a "cause" to develop into a major depressive episode.

In addition to counseling and medication, prayer therapy can be initiated. As described in the above examples, pray three times a day for a release from DEPRESSION. Then, wait while the warmth of God's love and His presence fills you. Finally, go about the remainder of the day, living as one who believes their prayer has been heard.

## Prayer for Release from DEPRESSION

"Oh gracious and kind heavenly Father, Holy is your name. I pray your kingdom may come to earth and complete your plan for our salvation. I pray, Father, you will cast out depression from my life and send it beyond the farthest mountain, never to return again. Forgive me when I have sabotaged my own well-being by not sleeping or eating in a health manner, by not forgiving others and myself, and by refusing to consider the medication that can help me. Open my eyes to your truths and let me discern what I can do to help myself, while I trust in you to help me. I pray you assist me in seeing beyond myself, so I may be kinder and gentler with others, lifting their spirits while lifting my own. Lead me not into self-pity, and deliver me from self-absorption. I acknowledge you have the power to heal even me, and I will sing your praises to others throughout my days. In the name of your son, my Lord, Jesus Christ, I pray. Amen."

## Control (of others)

Control is included in this brief list of conditions you may experience since it is the basis for many other problems, for example eating disorders and relational issues. Obviously, we all need to be in control of ourselves— controlling our temper, our behavior, and so on. However, when you blatantly try to control others, or become manipulative in order to control them, you display dysfunctional behavior. Sometimes, the consequence of controlling behavior can be life-threatening, such as attempting to control others by refusing to eat anything, or by throwing up what you ate minutes before.

Some people try to control others with displays of anger. Since they sense the other person is uncomfortable with anger, they give brilliant performances of rage in order to control them. The "controlee" wants to avoid the controller's display, so they give up and give in to the controller's desires or whims.

Some people attempt to control others by withholding love. They turn their back on their spouse or child, refusing to kiss them good-night and may even refuse to speak to them. Or, they are passive-aggressive with a non-display of anger or non-cooperation, by simply not-doing, non-everything.

"Will you take out the trash, Dear?"

"Sure." But they continue to watch TV or peck at the computer.

"We need to leave in five minutes, Honey."
"Okay. I'm almost ready." Meanwhile, thirty minutes later, they are still deciding what to wear.

Rather than an open discussion of a problem or pending possibilities, the controlling person manipulates the situation, controlling the others around him/her, by withholding themselves, or by not doing the very thing they said they would do.

Sometimes control can be very difficult to admit, especially to oneself, because control is so manipulative. People do not want to be manipulated and they certainly do not want to recognize manipulation in themselves.

The normal reaction to being manipulated is anger. Manipulators often don't understand why those around them are angry with them much of the time. The only way to rid oneself of controlling others through manipulative behavior is to first admit it.

Granted, control of others is not a basic emotion from which we suffer, like depression, anger, fear, etc. We control others when we suffer from fear and self-hating. We fear we will not belong unless we are controlling others.

They hate themselves for being so inadequate so they need to control others.

While we pray for the release of one negative emotion per week, we can pray for the surrender of control at the same time, since it is not an emotion.

**Prayer for Release of CONTROL (of Others)**

"Father in the high dwelling places and lover of my soul, I see your beautiful name written on the face of heaven. May your kingdom of peace and love come swiftly as you already rule in Heaven. It is very hard for me to admit that I try to control others but I see the results of my strangle hold on my loved ones. Please, release me from my need to control and manipulate others, in spite of my need to deny it. I turn control of my life and the lives of others, over to you. Lead me into the unknown and I will follow. Forgive me when I try to take back control and I pray I will be able to forgive others even more than they forgive me so I may not withhold any measure of compassion. Lead my feet swiftly past control's powerful clutch, for you are mightier than any force that may lure me from you. May my entire life be part of your kingdom and totally under your authority. I give you all praise and honor, now and forever more. In the dear name of my Lord and Savior, Jesus Christ, I pray. Amen."

In your quiet time, close your eyes and wait on the Lord. See yourself with a group of friends and family you have bound with rope, while you hold the tether's end. Then, see Jesus putting his hand on your shoulder, giving you the courage to let go of the rope. Allow the rope to loosen its grip on your loved ones until it finally falls to the floor. Jesus' hand remains on your shoulder, supporting you through any fear of loss of control. Feel his hand continuing to rest on your shoulder throughout the remainder of the day.

Chapter 16

**Intercession**

Intercession is prayer on behalf of someone else. These prayers may be for members of your family, your friends, community, country, or world— anyone or anything that is other than yourselves. We know that intercessory prayer works.

I once heard Dr. James Dobson speaking on television about a recent stroke he had experienced. He was assured by his physicians that the stroke was a very serious one. He could not see, speak, or move.

All over the world, millions of people joined in prayer on Dr. Dobson's behalf as he lay in his hospital room. Those prayers were answered as he quickly recovered with no lingering effects. His speech returned rapidly, as well as his sight, and his mobility. God is good and he does answer intercessory prayer.

I remember a young man, a senior at Taylor University, who had cancer. The entire University community prayed for his specific needs. His blood count had to rise to an exact numerical value before treatment could continue. His blood count did rise, to the exact number for which all were praying. He rallied and in the spring he graduated with his class. Not long after his graduation, he went home to Jesus. Why? I don't know. I do know God is good and he answers our prayers for others, as he answered our specific intercessory prayers for that young man.

Some years ago I saw an interview of an opera singer who had skin cancer on her beautiful face. She suffered after many operations to remove that cancer.

She told the interviewer that others had asked her if she ever questioned, "Why me?"

Her answer was, "Why not me?" Life happens.

We are to pray for others diligently and specifically. Let us remember others in our prayers. God is not our Santa Claus giving us only what we ask for ourselves. He is the God of all. Since prayers of intercession are specific prayers of petition, I have included them under the section of Petition. Using the model of the Lord's Prayer, a prayer of intercession could look like the following:

**A Prayer of Intercession**

"My father in the vast space of Heaven, I honor your sacred name. I pray your kingdom may come to earth so you may reign here as you do in heaven. Oh Father, I see the anger in my friend Jane's eyes, and know she must be churning with rage inside. I understand anger because I become angry too. But you, Father, are healing my soul of the anger that smolders inside me. Now, I ask you to visit Jane's heart and heal the torment that wells up inside of her and bring her your peace. I thank you for the healing you are accomplishing within me and I know you can heal Jane as well. Forgive me when I fail to stand behind your protective arm and try to face anger's ugly countenance on my own. Help me to forgive Jane completely when she lashes out in anger, for I know anger has her in its grip. You, oh Father, hold lightening in your hand; you can certainly hold my anger in check, as well as Jane's, for you are mighty beyond all power we have ever seen. This is your kingdom Lord, now and forever more and you reign in glory here in my heart. I pray to you, not out of any merit I have, but by the grace of Jesus' love and his worthiness. Amen."

Chapter 17

**Secret Prayer**

As a teenager, I saw the movie of Lloyd C. Douglas's *The Magnificent Obsession,* and again recently on television. The premise of the book and film was simple. A young doctor learned to give of himself and never ask for anything in return. Good deeds were never to be paid back. The gifts, the blessings, are never to be spoken of, only passed on to someone else, with the similar instructions: (1) never tell anyone, (2) never pay it back (3) and promise to pass it on. The favor, or good deed, cannot be paid back, because the "blessing has already been used."

The blessing was used up when the doctor was given the privilege of helping someone else. The doctor became "obsessed," or unable to stop doing "good" once he began a life of service. A new book and movie, *Pay It Forward,* makes the same request. Do not pay back the favor—pay it forward.

That idea has filled my soul with song ever since. It drives my energies and consumes my purpose. It is a sacred ministry, to have no purpose but the Lord's. What a magnificent obsession!

As a psychologist, I know what I do and what I say does have an impact on my clients. As a Christian, I know I make a difference in people's lives from time to time. Using the concept of the *Magnificent Obsession,* my purpose is to do God's will, in service to others.

This is my **Magnificat.** I pray each day to be of use to God, to say or do something that will benefit someone else . . . and . . . I do not want to know the circumstances under which I am of use, because (1) the glory belongs to God and (2) the blessing has already been used. The blessing was used up when I was given the privilege of being of use to God with one of his children. I want no clue as to when I was used.

The Bible tells us, when Jesus' healing energies were used by the woman who had been bleeding for years, as she touched him, he felt the energy leave him. I do not want to know when I have been used, when I have touched someone. It is my gift to God so I may not boast, "See what God and I have done."

I include this secret prayer at the end of each of my prayers, so my heart has been made right, and has been prepared for his use. I would like to challenge you to begin a magnificent journey of service by praying such a prayer of your own.

The prayer I use, that I challenge many of my clients in therapy to use, and that I give to you here, is:

"Father, may I be of use to you today? May I speak your words of comfort and encouragement to someone, or be of use to someone in some way, and may I not know when it happens, with whom it happens, or under what circumstances it happens. So you, Father God, receive all the glory, and so I am not corrupted into thinking it was anything that I did on my own. Amen."

**The Secret Prayer:**
**Included in a Prayer Therapy prayer for release from FEAR**

"Father, God, I know that you are the Holy One of Heaven who bends to live within your servants, so that we might live within you. May your kingdom of Love come quickly, within the plan you have for your people. For today, I ask that you release me from fear, for I know that fear is the basis of all the negative emotions that hold me captive. Throw my fear as far from me as the East is from the West, and may it never return. Forgive me when I react with anger to another's fear, because I should know their experience. Let me love them into wholeness.

May this be the day when you use me to touch one of your children with your healing hand. Or, may I say or do whatever they need, to sooth their troubled soul, and release them from the chains that bind. I only ask that you do not reveal who the person is, when it happens, or under what circumstances it happens. I want only for you to be lifted up, and that all glory is yours, Father. I do not want to try to boast about the work of the Holy Spirit in my life, as if I were the only one who has been blessed by your Holy visitation. In the name of your precious son, my redeemer, Jesus Christ, I pray. Amen"

The following pages are your opportunity to begin a prayer journal using your own words. I hope you will continue to use the Lord's Prayer format and Prayer Therapy. I pray you will consider a new way of life by using the Secret Prayer just described. God Bless you and your magnificent obsession in prayer.

Chapter 18

**A Prayer Journal**

We have looked at the components of prayer as taught by our Lord in the Lord's Prayer and I have coached you in the elements of Prayer Therapy and the Secret Prayer. Now, I want you to begin keeping a prayer journal. In a prayer journal, we list those for whom we pray and the emotions for which we pray for release. Date each prayer so you can remember the time and place you went to God in prayer. By doing this, you can later review your previous prayers and thank God for prayers heard and answered. You will marvel at the way in which God chose to answer your prayers, rather than being limited by your own narrow view of possible solutions.

Begin by creating some prayers, building them on the elements Jesus knew to be necessary. Include the Secret Prayer. We will use mostly Prayer Therapy during the Petition portion, since it is Prayer Therapy that we are learning. The Secret Prayer has been placed before the Closing.

However, if it is more appropriate for you to place the Secret Prayer in the beginning or middle of your prayer, feel free to do so. I will include a few prayers of Petition for others so you remember that others are included in your petitions.

If it is hard for you to remember others, then include a Petition for release from Selfishness for yourself, as you Petition God on behalf of others. If you tend to forget others, make sure you always include Petitions for others, since you do not naturally think of others.

"We must deliberately do what we do not naturally do."

Some therapy clients are concerned because they were not lavished with love when they were growing up. While they want to be more demonstrative with their own children, they find they do not know how. As Jean Ellsley Clarke described it, "They don't have the bone knowledge."

I encourage these parents to demonstrate love every day at regular intervals, such as, when their children awaken in the morning, after lunch, and before they go to bed at night. If they have to write a schedule and put it on the refrigerator, or enter a notation into their appointment book, they should do so. That sounds too mechanical to you? It is a matter of learning new habits. They certainly have a desire to demonstrate love. They just don't have the "bone knowledge."

In order to learn to perform new habits, you have to practice them. In order to practice them, you must deliberately do what is not your inclination to do, until the habit is established. Therefore, if it is not your habit to pray for others, then make it a practice to always pray for others during prayer time, so new habits can be established.

The following are some helpful outlines for you to use in prayer journaling as you continue in pray. There are several pages with examples of the outlined format. Next, there are pages with simple topic headings without suggestions.

You may want to start a loose leaf notebook for your prayer journal or you might enjoy one of the colorfully bound journal books with blank pages available in book stores. Whatever you decide to use for your prayer journal, the important issue is what goes inside, not how bright and lovely the binding. If you are reading this as an eBook, enter the headings as you go.

I strongly encourage you to write your own words on the lines provided, rather than simply copying the examples I have written. You may, of course, use my prayers at any time, but in this learning process, create your own prayers, forming each phrase with your own words. This will allow you to understand the Lord's Prayer and the process of prayer more deeply, and own your prayers more completely.

*Prayer Therapy of Jesus*                             Doris Gaines Rapp, Ph.D.

**Date:**

**Acknowledgment** (Example: Oh loving Father . . .)

*Your acknowledging statement:*


**Reverence/Worship** (Example: ... how amazing is your love.)

*Your statement of reverence and worship:*


**Pray for Christ's Return** (Example: May your Kingdom come swiftly to Earth)

*Your prayer statement for Christ's return to Earth:*


**Surrender** (Example: Take my life and mold it to your will.)

*Your prayer of surrender:*


**Petition - Prayer Therapy and Intercession** (Example: Oh Father, I feel so down today. Release me from the power depression has over my life today and set me free to be me.)

(Example: Father, my child is so rebellious today. Please, set her free from the grip that control has taken over her life, so she may not destroy herself while trying to control me. Help me to let her know she belongs even when she is not trying to control.)

*Your Prayer Therapy Petition for yourself:*


*Your Prayer of Petition for another:*

**Pray for Forgiveness** (Example: Father, forgive me for my selfishness and take away any desire or inclination toward selfishness in my life.)

*Your prayer for forgiveness:*

**Deliver Us From Sin** (Example: Father, may I not see the ease of deceit and please protect me from Satan's tempting lure.)

*Your prayer for deliverance from sin:*

**Acknowledging God's Omnipresence** (Example: Father I recognize you are everywhere and everywhere is yours.)

*Your statement of acknowledgment of God's Omnipresence:*

**Acknowledging God's Omnipotence** (Example: Father, I am weak but you are strong.)

*Your statement of recognition of God's Omnipotence:*

**Relinquishing Credit Back to God** (Example: To God be the glory for everything in my life.)

*Your relinquishment of credit back to God:*

**Secret Prayer** (Example: Father God, I humbly ask to be used by you today, but don't let me know when it happens, under what circumstances, or with whom it happens, so I may not boast.)

*Your Secret Prayer:*

**Claiming Christ's Power** (Example: I humbly pray in the name and by the power of Jesus Christ.)

*Your claim to the power of Jesus Christ:*


**Closing** (Example: Father, may it be so.)

*The closing of your prayer:*

*Prayer Therapy of Jesus*                         Doris Gaines Rapp, Ph.D.

**Date:**

**Acknowledgment** (Example: Our most gracious and kind heavenly father—)

*Your statement of acknowledgment:*


**Reverence/Worship** (Example: I bow before you.)

*Your statement of worship:*


**Pray for Christ's Return** (Example: May your kingdom be fulfilled as you promised.)

*Your prayer for Christ's return:*


**Surrender** (Example: Father, I give my life to you.)

*Your statement of surrender:*


**Petition - Prayer Therapy and Intercession** (Example: Oh Father, deliver me from selfishness so I may be of use to you.)

Example: Father God, my child is so depressed, carry him in your arms across the great abyss in his life and deliver him from depression and to health again.)

*Your Prayer Therapy Petition for yourself:*


*Your Prayer of Petition for another:*

**Prayer For Forgiveness** (Example: Father I pray for your forgiveness and ask that you place forgiveness for (name) heavily on my heart.)

*Your prayer for forgiveness:*


**Deliver Us From Sin** (Example: Father, deliver me from the craving for chocolate.)

*Your prayer for deliverance from sin:*


**Acknowledging God's Omnipresence** (Example: We are your people, tending your world, since all is yours.)

*Your acknowledgment of God's Omnipresence:*


**Acknowledging God's Omnipotence** (Example: Father, all power in heaven and on earth belongs to you.)

*Your statement of acknowledgment of the Omnipotence of God:*


**Relinquishing Credit Back To God** (Example: All glory and honor and praise are yours, Father, not mine. It belongs rightly to you.)

*Your relinquishment of credit back to God:*


**Secret Prayer** (Example: Oh Father, may I be your hands, your feet, your voice for someone in need today. Please hide my eyes and ears from knowledge of my helping you, for I truly want only you to shine through.)

*Your Secret Prayer:*

**Claiming Christ's Power** (Example: In the precious name of Jesus and the power of his son-ship.)

*Your opportunity to claim Christ's power through the authority of his name:*


**Closing** (Example: May my words and plans be your words and plans, your words and plans my words and plans.)

*Your closing statement:*

*Prayer Therapy of Jesus* — Doris Gaines Rapp, Ph.D.

**Date:**

**Acknowledgment:**

**Reverence/Worship:**

**Prayer for Christ's Return:**

**Surrender:**

**Petition (Prayer Therapy and Intercession):**

**Prayer for Forgiveness:**

**Deliverance from Our Sins:**

**Acknowledge God's Omnipresence:**

**Acknowledge God's Omnipotence:**

**Relinquishing Back to God:**

**Claiming Christ's Power:**

**Secret Prayer:**

**Closing:**

**Date:**

**Acknowledgment:**

**Reverence/Worship:**

**Prayer for Christ's Return:**

**Surrender:**

**Petition (Prayer Therapy and Intercession):**

**Prayer for Forgiveness:**

**Deliver Us From Our Sins:**

**Acknowledgment of God's Omnipresence:**

**Acknowledgment of God's Omnipotence:**

**Relinquishing Credit Back to God:**

**Claiming Christ's Power:**

**Secret Prayer:**

**Closing:**

*Prayer Therapy of Jesus*   Doris Gaines Rapp, Ph.D.

**Date:**

**Acknowledgment:**

**Reverence/Worship:**

**Prayer for Christ's Return:**

**Surrender:**

**Petition (Prayer Therapy and Intercession):**

**Prayer for Forgiveness:**

**Deliver Us From Our Sins:**

**Acknowledging God's Omnipresence:**

**Acknowledgment of God's Omnipotence:**

**Relinquishing Credit Back to God:**

**Claiming Christ's Power:**

**Secret Prayer:**

**Closing:**

*Prayer Therapy of Jesus*   Doris Gaines Rapp, Ph.D.

**Date:**

**Acknowledgment:**

**Reverence/Worship:**

**Prayer for Christ's Return:**

**Surrender:**

**Petition (Prayer Therapy and Intercession):**

**Deliverance from Our Sins:**

**Acknowledge God's Omnipresence:**

**Acknowledge God's Omnipotence:**

**Relinquishing Back to God:**

**Claiming Christ's Power:**

**Secret Prayer:**

**Closing:**

*Prayer Therapy of Jesus*                    Doris Gaines Rapp, Ph.D.

**Date:**

**Acknowledgment:**

**Reverence/Worship:**

**Prayer for Christ's Return:**

**Surrender:**

**Petition (Prayer Therapy and Intercession):**

**Prayer for Forgiveness:**

**Deliverance from Our Sins:**

**Acknowledge God's Omnipresence:**

**Acknowledge God's Omnipotence:**

**Relinquishing Back to God:**

**Claiming Christ's Power:**

**Secret Prayer:**

**Closing:**

*Prayer Therapy of Jesus*                                        Doris Gaines Rapp, Ph.D.

**Date:**

**Acknowledgment:**

**Reverence/Worship:**

**Prayer for Christ's Return:**

**Surrender:**

**Petition (Prayer Therapy and Intercession):**

**Prayer for Forgiveness:**

**Deliverance from Our Sins:**

**Acknowledge God's Omnipresence:**

**Acknowledge God's Omnipotence:**

**Relinquishing Back to God:**

**Claiming Christ's Power:**

**Secret Prayer:**

**Closing:**

Chapter 19

**Go Forth**

Now go forth in prayer. Go out into the world and carry the love and healing power of God with you as you pray for others, so God may work his miracles in their lives. In some part of your prayers you'll be praying for release from specific negative aspects of yourself—your "Prayer Therapy" prayers. During other moments of prayer, you'll be praying specifically for others—"prayers of intercession." At the end, as you prepare to go forth, you'll be praying a secret prayer of service.

It must be secret or it is not your ministry. If you are sincere in your desire to be of service to God, you would not be able to give me a single reason why anyone should know that help came through you. It would be your sole desire to lift up the Lord so he may be glorified—a truly magnificent journey! May his blessings be with you as you seek to do his work while glorifying Him.

**REFERENCES**

Clarke, Jean Ellsley (1985). *Self-Esteem a Family Affair*. Harper. San Francisco.

Douglas, Lloyd C. (1938). *Magnificent Obsession*. HM.

Lucado, Max (1996). *In the Grip of Grace*. Word Publishing, Dallas, Texas.

Parker, William R. and St. Johns, Elaine (1957). *Prayer Can Change Your Life*. Prentice Hall Press, New York.

Hyde, Catherine (2000). *Pay It Forward*. Simon & Schuster. New York.

Smedes, Lewis B. (1984). *Forgive and Forget*. Harper & Row, Publishers, Inc. New York. Also: Pocket Books, New York.

*Webster's New Collegiate Dictionary* (1975). G. & C. Merriam- Webster, Springfield, Massachusetts

## ABOUT THE AUTHOR

**Doris Gaines Rapp, Ph.D.**

Author, psychologist, speaker, and former educator, Doris Gaines Rapp, Ph.D. has directed the Counseling Centers at Taylor University, in Upland and Bethel College in Mishawaka, Indiana. Rapp has enjoyed spending the last two years as a full time writer and is the author of four novels and three non-fiction books, all available to be ordered from neighborhood bookstores and online. A fifth novel will be out in the early winter. Her work with Prayer Therapy is posted each Monday on her blog: www.prayertherapyrapp.blogspot.com.

Dr. Rapp has been aware of restlessness in the community of believers that is not quenched by material possessions or experimentation, as in "church hopping." People seem to be searching for "the one"—the one to save them from themselves—the one to heal. The search is over! Healing was brought to earth 2000 years ago by the "great physician."

Dr. Rapp teaches Prayer Therapy, as a means to access that healing, in her writing and through speaking engagements. She and her husband, Rev. Bill Rapp, have survived the rearing of six children. They live in Indiana.

## Other Books by Doris Gaines Rapp

(2014) *Christmas Feathers* – A short story, prequel to *Smoke from Distant Fires*. In a compilation of short stories from eight authors, titled *Christmases Past*
(2013) *Escape from the Belfry*
(2014) *Hiawassee – Child of the Meadow*
(2013) *Length of Days – The Age of Silence* [2$^{nd}$ Ed]
(2015) *Lent is for Giving In, Not Giving Up*
    This Lent Devotional will be available in the spring
(2014) *Smoke from Distant Fires*
(2014) *Waiting for Jesus in a Can't Wait World – Advent*

All of these books can be ordered from www.amazon.com, www.cokesbury.com, www.barnesandnoble.com. Or, you can order them from your local bookstore.

**Internet Presence:**

www.dorisgainesrapp.com
www.dorisgainesrapp.blogspot.com
www.prayertherapyrapp.blogspot.com
https://www.amazon.com/author/dorisgainesrapp
Facebook.com/pages/Doris-Gaines-Rapp-Author-Page

www.ingramcontent.com/pod-product-compliance
Lightning Source LLC
Chambersburg PA
CBHW050557300426
44112CB00013B/1958